DATE DUE

Desire and Its Discontents

Desire and Its Discontents

EUGENE GOODHEART

Columbia University Press
New York

Columbia University Press
New York   Oxford

Copyright © 1991 Columbia University Press

Library of Congress Cataloging-in-Publication Data
Goodheart, Eugene.
    Desire and its discontents / Eugene Goodheart.
        p.   cm.
    Includes index.
    ISBN 0-231-07642-8 : $35.00
    1. Desire in literature.   2. Desire.   3. Fiction—19th century—
History and criticism.   4. Fiction—20th century—History and
criticism.   I. Title.
PN56.D48G6   1991
809.3′9353—dc20   92-23243
                                                                        CIP

∞

Casebound editions of Columbia University Press books are Smyth-sewn
and printed on permanent and durable acid-free paper.

Printed in the United States of America

c 10 9 8 7 6 5 4 3 2 1

ᴈ❧ Contents

Contents

?• Acknowledgments

I want to thank Daniel Aaron, Werner Berthoff, Morris Dick-
stein, Alvin Kibel, and Robert Nozick for their careful and helpful
readings of the manuscript. This is not the first time that their
suggestions have improved what I have written and I hope not the
last. During the academic year 1987–88, the National Humanities
Center provided me with collegial fellowship and the ideal circumstances for work. I spent August 1989 at the Rockefeller Founda-
tion's Villa Serbelloni, where my work prospered. I am grateful to
both staffs for their wonderful support.

Earlier versions of a number of chapters appeared in journals:
chapter 4 in *Antaeus*, chapter 6 in *Explorations*, chapter 7 in *Partisan Review*. Passages from essays written for *Contemporary Literature* and *South Atlantic Quarterly* appear in chapters 1 and 9. A
version of chapter 5 appeared in the June 1988 issue and is re-
printed from *The World and I*, a publication of The Washington

Times Corporation, copyright (c) 1988. I am grateful to the editors for permisson to reprint material from their journals.

I should also thank my hosts at the University of Colorado, Harvard University, the University of North Carolina (Chapel Hill), the University of South Florida, the University of Southwestern Louisiana, Stanford University, and Tulane University for opportunities to lecture on my subject at their institutions and benefit from the give and take of discussion.

I want to express my appreciation to Elaine Herrmann for her admirably efficient and patient typing of a manuscript written in a longhand that wasn't always reader friendly.

My wife Joan Bamberger's keen intelligence and eye for sense and absurdity helped me keep my bearings. Her criticisms, delivered with humor and affection, made the writing and rewriting enjoyable.

Desire and Its Discontents

❧ Introduction: What We Talk About When We Talk About Desire

Desire is a manifestation of life itself—of all of life, and it encompasses everything from reason down to scratching oneself. —DOSTOEVSKY

Reason is, and ought only to be the slave of the passions. —HUME

Reason is no more than the state of the relations between passions and desires . . . every passion contains in itself its own quantum of reason. —NIETZSCHE

In the struggle between reason and desire, the philosophical tradition from Plato to Kant has given the prize to reason. Reason ought to rule desire. The quotations above form a counter-tradition, its origins are in the modern period. This counter-tradition inverts the hierarchy of desire and reason, or alternatively, dissolves the distinction altogether, saying in effect that desire is everything: it generates and consumes all of life. In recent years there has been an explosion of talk about desire, drawing on this counter-tradition, that has challenged the values of rationalist discourse, in particular the rationalist model of the self. Coherence, unity, wholeness—the value terms of that discourse—have been transformed into terms of repression. What is repressed is desire,

1

which has come to stand for freedom or for the thing that needs to be liberated. What is desire?

The word is so basic to our lives, so much part of our everyday speech, akin to words like "want" and "need" that it may seem pedantic to ask for a definition of it. What is striking, however, is the way the word in what I call the discourse of desire resists definition. Leo Bersani begins his book *A Future for Astyanax: Character and Desire in Literature* by acknowledging "a certain blurring of conceptual boundaries" in his use of the word. "As I use that word, it obviously has affinities with the eighteenth-century notion of enthusiasm, with the concept of vision in Milton and Blake as well as in English romantic criticism." He prefers "desire" to "vision" or "freedom" because of what he considers to be the "idealistic associations and contexts" of the latter terms. He believes that a psychoanalytically oriented use of the term "desire" will clarify what he is most interested in: "adventures in psychic mobility." And he eschews a "rigorous technical study of desire," because he wants the flexibility to adapt it to the various texts he addresses in his book.[1]

Bersani's willfulness is not capricious. It is a function of the word itself, or at least of a particular conception of the word. As an advocate of desire Bersani wishes to have his critical practice illustrate the elusive energies it aims to discover in the various texts. To trap desire within clearly defined conceptual boundaries would destroy, so to speak, its very essence. From this perspective, desire may be understood as an energy of negation. In her essay "The Ethics of Linguistics," Julia Kristeva speaks of ethical codes that "must be shattered in order to give way to the free play of negativity, need, desire and jouissance."[2] In linguistic terms, desire signifies an unstable and aggressive energy that disintegrates structures of reason, self, morality, convention, all attempts to contain and fix reality. It becomes a motive of a radical linguistic skepticism.

Now this is not what we ordinarily mean by the word. In its vernacular expressions, we desire particular satisfactions: food, sex, pleasure, happiness. But the word, when used by writers like Bersani and Kristeva, does not require a predicate. Desire moves, floats, negates, shatters, aspires, it is itself a subject. Its freedom, if that is what we wish to call it, consists in its refusal to be constrained by the satisfactions that would extinguish it. Does this constitute freedom? Is Desire (in the grand categorical sense in which it is currently employed) a legitimate signifier of liberation and freedom? I am calling a fundamental assumption of this discourse of desire into question.[3]

But how do we propose to answer the question, if the word refuses to stay put? The elusiveness and indefinability of desire and of its objects, I believe, have a specific character. Few, if any, imaginative writers have explored the career of desire with more rigor and honesty than Proust and he has done so without obliterating its aura of mystery. It may be instructive to consider what Marcel, the narrator of *Remembrance of Things Past,* has to say about that career. For him desire lives not in the world, but in the imagination. He speaks of "my imagination drawing strength from contact with my sensuality, my sensuality expanding through all the realms of my imagination, my desire no longer had any bounds."* Even if objects offer themselves for satisfaction they are bound to disappoint, because "a person in flesh and blood" contains "so little of our dream" (2:700). The gap between desire and its object is insurmountable. Indeed, it is the very gap that nourishes and sustains desire, because its satisfaction would be its extinction. It may even court rejection, since denial only increases desire. Desire is committed to permanent revolution, to an enduring disappointment as a way of guaranteeing its survival.

Desire exists beyond need. Need is determinate, it demands and achieves satisfaction: it expresses man's animal nature. Desire is a "spiritual" energy; it "represents" the indefinable in human life. In a religious sense, it has as its object identification with the will of God. Desire does not disappear with the disappearance of God, but becomes necessarily insatiable. As Dostoevsky well knew, only a God worthy of devotion could chasten desire and make it satiable. "Modern" desire persists in the wake of the disappearance of God. All definitions of it are always premature and, to one degree of another, preemptive. Desire is ruled by mystery. Proust again is our authority in this matter. "Desire for people . . . ends in anxiety . . . having for its object a being at once unknown and

---

* Marcel Proust, *Remembrance of Things Past,* translated by C. K. Scott Moncrieff (New York: Random House, 1924–1934), 1:20. Subsequent references have been indicated with volume and page numbers in the text that follows.

unconscious" (1:541). For this reason, philosophers in their wisdom "recommend us to set limits to our desires." We want what we cannot know and cannot have. "We love only what we do not possess" (2:648). Knowledge and possession are the death of desire. "The farther the desire advances, the farther does true possession withdraw." The subject, however, does not settle for mystery, but seeks to know and possess even if the pursuit is futile. And the reason that the pursuit is futile is that he can never really "emerge from himself," he can know "his fellows only in himself" (2:698). Indeed, he has only himself, his subjectivity, because objects (in this case, other subjects, people) forever elude him. To be sure, desire requires the illusion that "there is a reality which conforms to it, even if, for us, it is not to be realized" (1:539). On occasion, Proust appears to contradict himself when he declares, for instance, that "the possession of what we love is an even greater joy than love itself" (2:413). We may wonder, however, whether Proust is speaking here of actual possession or of the illusion of possession.

Why should the desiring subject seek to perpetuate the suffering of deprivation? Proust answers for the writer: "Desire is not without its value to the writer in detaching him first of all from his fellow men and from conforming to their standards, and afterwards in restoring some degree of movement to a spiritual machine which, after a certain age, tends to become paralyzed" (2:506). Even more affirmingly, he associates the creative spirit with "the full extent of suffering. And the most terrible reality brings us, with our suffering, the joy of a great discovery" (2:367).

Desire is a mode of cognition (self-discovery), since it projects "into [the beloved object] a state of our own soul. . . . The important thing is, therefore, not the worth of the woman but the depth of the state; and that the emotions which a young girl of no kind of distinction arouses in us can enable us to bring to the surface of our consciousness some of the most intimate parts of our being, more personal, more remote, more essential than would be reached by the pleasure that we derive from the conversation of a great man or even from the admiring contemplation of his work" (1:627). A question remains whether the illusory terms of this kind of self-discovery (wherein we believe that we see the other when we see only a reflection of ourselves) does not contaminate the knowledge that we have presumably obtained. And if the desiring subject proves to be as lacking or even empty as the object of desire (certainly the case if "we exist only by virtue of what we possess" [2:725]), what then is to be gained from desire?

If not knowledge of the self, which becomes as multiple, as elusive as the object of desire, perhaps knowledge of desire itself is possible. Suffering and joy, sorrow and happiness become indistinguishable in the career of desire. How can we sort out the sources of happiness and suffering in the following passage?

> . . . What makes us so happy is the presence in our heart of an unstable element which we are perpetually arranging to keep in position, and of which we cease almost to be aware so long as it is not displaced. Actually, there is in love a permanent strain of suffering which happiness neutralizes, makes conditional only, procrastinates, but which may at any moment become what it would long since have been had we not obtained what we were seeking, sheer agony. (1:443)

In both the "instability of the heart" and the effort to immobilize it (so that our beloved will not be displaced) there is joy and pain. Desire is an emotional shuttle which depends upon a conflict of emotion. ". . . And it was consequently her whole life that filled me with desire; a sorrowful desire because I felt that it was not to be realized, but exhilarating, because what had hitherto been my life, having ceased of a sudden to be my whole life, being no more now than a little part of the space stretching out before me, which I was burning to cover and which was composed of the lives of these girls, offered me that prolongation, that possible multiplication of oneself which is happiness" (1:600).

In Roland Barthes, one of Proust's most brilliant contemporary epigones, we find repeated confirmations of the Proustian conception of desire. "In reality, it is unimportant that I have no likelihood of being *really* fulfilled. . . . Only the will to fulfillment shines, indestructible, before me. By this will, I well up: I form within myself the utopia of a subject free from repression."[4] This is the imaginative expression of desire, insulated from the impositions of reality. But Barthes, who is less confident than Proust of his own imaginative power, experiences more than Proust the pathos, the impoverishment of the desiring subject. The object of desire proves to be no more than a metonym, a fetishistic part of the beloved. "Aside from these fetishes, there is no other object in the amorous world. It is a world sensuously impoverished, abstract, erased, canceled out."[5] The condition of the desiring subject is pure narcissism. "Me! And me! What about me!" The lover is "flung back on the solipsism of [his] discourse."[6]

The only justification of illimitable desire (as both Proust and Barthes know) is the imagination. Desire is the source of narrative. It generates the obstacles it must overcome or circumvent through ruses, deceptions, and displacements. It creates the devious shapes of narrative by aiming for satisfaction, deferring it and discovering its satisfaction as well as agony in deferral. And the deferral of satisfaction as a permanent condition paradoxically makes possible "the multiplication of oneself which is happiness."

Is there an object that if possessed would give ultimate satisfaction? A psychoanalytic perspective necessarily focuses on Marcel's relations with his mother and the trauma of her "abandonment" of him, the episode of her failure one night to appear in his bedroom to kiss him goodnight. The episode reverberates throughout the novel. The Oedipal object of desire then would be the mother with whom union or reunion is always impossible. From a psychoanalytic point of view, the girls Marcel pursues (Odile, Gilberte, Albertine) are displacements, inevitably inadequate substitutes for the mother. The narrative of *Remembrance of Things Past* can be conceived as a construction of the failed repetitious enactments of the desire for the mother.

In *Beyond the Pleasure Principle*, Freud engages the difficult phenomenon of repetition compulsion. In his examination of the case of the infant who responded to his mother's daily departure by a ritual of repeated casting out and retrieving of his cotton reel, Freud discovered the unconscious motive of mastering the anxiety of the departure and return of the mother. In performing that act, the child in a sense controls the mother's departure and return. According to Lacan, "desire must insistently repeat itself until it be recognized."[7] But the recognition of desire does not in Marcel's case entail mastery. His desire survives every recognition. According to Serge Doubrovsky, "the system, of narrative discontinuities that structure the Proustian novel . . . enables the Narrator to master his deep anxiety vis-à-vis the inexplicable coming and going of the Other, while leaving intact the Other's arbitrary and lacunal quality . . . the writer . . . strives for the liberation which the whole book shows to be constantly escaping our grasp."[8] And he goes on to characterize Proust's work as "completely inscribed within the structure of neuroses. . . . Far from being a *deliverance* from that structure, his work attests to it as a truth that cannot be transcended."[9] One might add, even if one comes to know it.

The psychoanalytic perspective confirms the compulsive character of the career of desire. And it locates its true object in the displacements of that career. In effect, it explains why desire must be in ignorance of its object, why it must repress the knowledge. What psychoanalysis fails to do, I think, is to appreciate fully its mystery. It completely secularizes desire, resisting in its demystifying way its religious-aesthetic dimension. By placing the work within the structure of a medical pathology, the psychoanalytic perspective denies it any autonomous or separate aesthetic existence, that is, its capacity to transcend in imagination, if not in life, transcendence being the "flight" of the imagination itself. Proust understands the double contradictory movement of the imagination to unveil the truth and to preserve the sense of mystery. "We are attracted by every form of life which represents to us something unknown and strange, by a last illusion still unshattered"(1:1120). Psychoanalysis or any analysis cannot adequately represent the enlivening power of desire in writing.

Desire "alone makes us take an interest in the existence and character of another person" (2:430). It empowers the imagination, leads it to joy and sorrow, but confines itself to imagination. Lived out in the world, it would destroy the self. Lacan has understood this Proustian insight in linguistic terms. For Lacan (in Ellie Ragland-Sullivan's words) "desire is the proof of a real castration."[10] Unlike the utopians of desire Deleuze and Guattari and before them Marcuse and Brown, he envisages no satisfaction in the real, because desire is eternally alienated from the real, its satisfaction impossible. And yet within the realm of language (or imagination), desire may cross the limit of the pleasure principle and experience a tragic intensity of being that makes for affirmation. The exemplary heroes and heroines of Lacanian psychoanalysis are the characters of tragedy on the order of Oedipus, Antigone, and Lear, heroes of the impossible who have deliberately entered the region of desire and suffering, writing, in order to experience the fullest intensity of being.

The Proustian story is consistent with the prototypical modernist narrative. From the writer's point of view, the modernist narrative can be the acting out of desire, the courting of suffering and death. In *Death in Venice, Heart of Darkness, The Metamorphosis, The Immoralist,* the authors Mann, Conrad, Kafka, Gide, though they *write* their deaths in the figures of Aschenbach, Kurtz, Gregor Samsa, and Michel, respectively, survive their surrogate counterparts. Modernist writing expresses and testifies to a life that cannot be truly lived or can be lived only at great peril. One lesson of classic modern fiction may be summed up in a passage from Georges Bataille: "Life is essentially extravagant, drawing on its forces and reserves unchecked, it annihilates what it has created. . . . The thing we desire most is the most likely to drag us into wild extravagance and to ruin us."[11] Or in the following passage from Durkheim's famous study of *Suicide:* "Unlimited desires are insatiable by definition and insatiability is rightly considered a sign of morbidity. Being unlimited, they constantly and infinitely surpass the means at their command; they cannot be quenched. Inextinguishable thirst is constantly renewed torture."[12] Unlimited desire is what Schopenhauer called the will. Thomas Mann, writing about Schopenhauer, characterizes the will "as the opposite pole of passive satisfaction," it "is a fundamental unhappiness, it is unrest, a striving for *something*—it is want, cravings, avidity, demand, and a world of will can be nothing but a world of suffering."[13] Desire may be the condition of imaginative happiness, but it also may be "a world of suffering."

The desiring subject does not lack for everything; on the contrary, a condition of his desiring is a certain power and, as Bataille remarks, a capacity for extravagance. "No matter how one acts," Durkheim writes, "desires have to depend upon resources to some extent, actual possessions are partly the criterion of those aspired to. So the less one has the less one is tempted to extend the range of one's needs indefinitely. Lack of power, compelling moderation, accustoms men to it, while nothing excites envy if no one has superfluity. Wealth, on the other hand, by the power it bestows, deceives us into believing that we depend on ourselves only. Reducing the resistance we encounter from objects, it suggests the possibility of unlimited success against them. The less limited one feels, the more intolerable all limitation appears."[14] However baffled the imagination may be in its desire to know and possess its object, it cannot plead poverty or, if it does plead poverty, it is not to be believed for, as Durkheim points out, it already possesses the resources which enable it to dream of unrealized possibilities. For this reason morbidity is not the whole story. Empowering the imagination, desire enhances the experience of a life that it will also destroy. The modernist imagination ambiguously affirms and resists the claim of desire, and it does so by dividing writing from living.

The modernist representation of desire, which separates writing from living, has been challenged by certain postmodern critics, for example, Leo Bersani, who writes:

> Personality in Proust disintegrates as a result of excesses of verbal inspiration. The Proustian narrator exuberantly attacks his own coherence and allows himself the luxury of *being* the multiple desiring perspectives on the world which he discovers while writing. Such self-multiplication is explicitly the work of literature, and the narrator can perhaps afford to indulge it because he knows that the excesses of literature are always contained within the coherent system of a language. Being is exploded, made discontinuous and multiplied in Proust within a field of great compositional security.[15]

Bersani, however, is not content with the compositional limits imposed on the adventure in multiplication and self-fragmentation. "Proust eludes the more fundamental impulse to live or to die by the identification he makes between life-producing processes and the productive resources of literary metaphor." Proust eludes this impulse, because he understands the value of desire for writing and its destructiveness in life. Proust shows the cautionary wisdom of the realist about the dangers of excessive imagination.

> My jealousy was born of mental images, a form of self-torment not based upon probability. Now there may occur in the lives of men and of nations (and there was to occur, one day, in my own life) a moment when we need to have within us a superintendent of police, a clear-sighted diplomat, a master detective, who instead of pondering over the concealed possibilities that extend to all points of the compass, reasons accurately, says to himself: "If Germany announces this, it means that she intends to do something else, not just 'something' in the abstract, but precisely this or that or the other. . . ." (2:394)

9

A moment's reflection should make clear the reason for Bersani's discontent. If Proust has disintegrated the self within his novel, he has in a sense betrayed the cause of transgression and fragmentation by respecting the boundaries that separate writing from living. Coherence and closure have reinstalled themselves in the privileging of the compositional space. Bersani's criticism reenacts a characteristic postmodernist predilection for allowing the imagination to spill over into reality (Norman Mailer, William Burroughs are instances), to transgress the boundaries that normally separate writing from living. (Bersani concedes that "desublimated desire" is possible only in literature and that "to live entirely without sublimation and psychic continuities is unthinkable." But this statement at the end of his book seems to be a reluctant concession to reality, which for Bersani is the terror principle. "But we might argue that even the structured self can enter that play of mobile desire without which any project of radical self-revision runs the risk of merely changing the mode in which the self seeks terroristically to impose its desire on the world."[16] Note here how desire, the desire of the coherent self, functions as repression.)

Unless desire can enter the real, the self is doomed to an irreparable division between the mind and the body. In *Notes from Underground,* the protagonist argues for desire against reason or, more accurately, against the opposition between desire and reason in which reason asserts its superiority. The project of desire, as the underground man conceives it, is the recovery of "flesh and blood" reality from the unliving world of books. The underground man laments the modern condition.

> Why, today we don't even know where real life is, what it is, or what it's called! Left alone without literature, we immediately become entangled and lost—we don't know what to join, what to keep up with; what to love, what to hate; what to respect, what to despise! We even find it painful to be men—real men of flesh and blood, with *our own private bodies.*[17]

In *Remembrance of Things Past,* desire may mobilize a spiritual machine tending toward paralysis, but it also separates the imagination from "flesh and blood reality." Desire lives not in the body, but in literature. For the underground man, this division is a fatal modern condition, but the facts of his own life read like a parody of Proustian desire. The underground man's fantasies are completely bookish, utterly devoid of reality. Like Marcel, he is bound to an unknown object which he can never possess.

The dialectic of desire in *Notes from Underground* is surprising. In rebellion against a despotic utilitarian reason that deprives the individual of his personal identity, in effect reducing him to a "cipher, a statistic," an instance of the laws of nature, the underground man affirms the authenticity and freedom of being through desire. Utilitarianism appeals to what people desire as the arbiter of human behavior, but desire is already assimilated to social reason: "the greatest happiness for the greatest number." By circumscribing the area of desire as the pursuit of socially benign (or at least harmless) pleasure, utilitarianism transforms desire into an instrument of social reason. Desire becomes complicit in its own repression. The underground man forecloses the possibility of reading utilitarianism as involving a rational and liberating discrimination of desires in the interest of the desiring subject and his or her gratifications.

Dostoevsky's tale, both discursively and dramatically, "deconstructs" this assumed fraternity between reason and desire in the utilitarian view.

> Desire, of course, can if it wishes, agree with reason, especially if one uses it sparingly, never going too far. The desire is quite useful, even praiseworthy. But in reality, desire usually stubbornly disagrees with reason . . . and . . . let me tell you that this too is useful and praiseworthy.[18]

The underground man's counterexample to the utilitarian view is the man who with full knowledge of where his true interests (i.e., his pleasures) lie may deliberately seek an object which goes against his normal interests. He may seek suffering rather than pleasure. And the "reason" lies in what may be his deepest desire, the desire for individual freedom.

The effect of this "deconstruction" is the transformation of the nature of desire and its object. The desire for pleasure comes to be seen as a construction of reason and therefore inauthentic. Recall Dostoevsky's redefinition of desire: "Desire . . . is the manifestation of life itself—of all of life, and it encompasses everything from reason down to scratching oneself."[19] This new inclusiveness or illimitability of desire subordinates pleasure to suffering: "a man will never give up true suffering" which means doubt and "denial" and "chaos and destructiveness."[20]

In "The Fate of Pleasure," Lionel Trilling remarks that Nietzsche and Dostoevsky had conspired to devalue pleasure in the interest of a spiritual idea of suffering.[21] They have severed the traditional hedonist association of desire with pleasure. The coupling of Nietzsche and Dostoevsky is a familiar interpretive gesture, originating with Nietzsche himself. The paradox of the coupling consists in the apparent spiritual opposition between the two writers: Dostoevsky, the Christian, Nietzsche, the Antichrist. They share, despite the opposition, the experience and understanding of a resentment born of an insecurity about the sentiment of existence. To desire suffering as intensely as both the underground man and Nietzsche desire it bespeaks a need to feel alive against everything in the world that conspires to deny one's existence. Pleasure is a weak form of life, contaminated by its association with reason. The sentiment of nonexistence, it should be said at once, is not the same as death, since it accompanies an intense consciousness of one's nonexistence (a condition that the underground man repeatedly testifies to). Indeed, the desirable alternative to the *passion* of suffering, the sentiment of existence, is death, the irreversible extinction of consciousness. Thus Nietzsche can at once desire more life (suffering) and death (the extinction of consciousness). What he and the underground man cannot abide is the intermediate condition of consciousness in the mind and *in*existence in the body —a condition that can be characterized as death in life. For the underground man, the experience of suffering is the experience of reality and the guarantor of authenticity.

The association between desire and authenticity implicit in Dostoevsky's narrative can be understood in a sociopolitical perspective. The underground man, as an authorial footnote makes clear, is a type specific to a particular time and place. "People like the author of these notes may, and indeed must, exist in our society, if we think of the circumstances under which the society has been formed."[22] It becomes evident as we read that the underground man is the notorious alienated city intellectual, intensely conscious of the deficiencies and deprivations of his existence. (The underground man refers to Petersburg as "the most abstract of cities.") And the most painful deprivation that he experiences, more painful than physical hunger, is the absence of acknowledgment of his existence by others, which is the source of self-esteem. In his relations with friends, with the army officer, with his servant, what is at stake is the question of his existence: a question, because he cannot—his way of life does not permit him to—take his existence for granted. ("[The officer] grabbed me by the shoulders and, without a word, picked me up and setting me down a bit further away, passed by as if I didn't exist. I could've forgiven anything including a beating, but that was too much—to be brushed aside without being noticed!"[23] The underground man does not belong to the lower classes (he has a man servant), but he shares with the lower classes the sense of exclusion and anonymity; his superior origins may have given him a sense of pride (albeit thwarted), which inspires him to revolt, desire being the rebellious element in the politics of the psyche.

If desire *means* personal identity or freedom for the underground man, it does not follow that desire *is* freedom and identity. Desire in *Notes from Underground* turns out to be a species of compulsion. The underground man's suffering proves to be as compulsive as the normal man's desire for pleasure. His "psychic mobility" is unfree. In *Notes from Underground* the association between desire and freedom or life itself proves illusory. Desire in Dostoevsky's story functions as an unredeemable compulsive force, unlike the suffering of a Christian sinner, which may be redeemed.

What reads like necessity in Dostoevsky and Proust is choice or the avoidance of choice for Bersani who imagines a real condition of desire as "the luxury of being" in multiplicity. Bersani, I believe, has chosen to make a utopian appropriation of the Proustian experience. Is it a matter of choice if desire unchecked can ruin and destroy us? (In a sense, one has no choice in what one desires. A temperament inclined to illimitable desire may find it irresistible. But an ideology that promulgates desire as a supreme value has the effect of imposing an imperative upon those whose capacities for desire, whose desire to desire are limited. A person may choose to resist the impositions of such an ideology when he becomes conscious of its operations.) Moreover, even Bersani's apparently benign characterization of Proust's imaginative élan carries a suggestion of violence that cannot be easily reconciled with the utopian image of desire. He describes Proust's "verbal inspiration" not as a representation but as an action, provoked by the excesses of verbal inspiration, against the self.

To assault the coherent self is presumably to free oneself from all restraints, to win for oneself an unlimited freedom and power. Freedom and power: the discourse of desire is a political discourse. Milan Kundera's *The Unbearable Lightness of Being* is a particularly revealing meditation on the relationship between desire and power, in particular the relation between sexual desire and totalitarian politics. I want to take a long look at what it has to say about that relationship.

If erotic desire were an emblem of the anarchic self, one might expect eros to be inimical to all forms of tyranny. And indeed, totalitarian societies in particular are notoriously puritanical, because they fear the freedom represented by the erotic life. The erotic life may become the political arena of the artist, the most powerful and intimate expression of his or her selfhood. The artist is the natural enemy of despotism. The fear that despotic regimes exhibit toward artists must seem like sheer paranoia, if the threat is measured in conventional political terms. For what can the lone artist, even with his powerful imagination, hope to achieve against the all-powerful state? The province of the artist is precisely the one area in which the regime of politics is always insecure: the self, personal desire, and fantasy. The anarchic self, which the poet has the capacity to imagine (and perhaps enact), constitutes political insubordination, a refusal to accept the oppressive rules of social and political order. It is precisely the capacity of the self to preserve its freedom from *conventional* tyrannies that accounts for the totalitarian project, which is to conquer the last stronghold of freedom, the self. And it does so by "educating" the self to be complicit with its aims. The aim of totalitarian control is self-domination.

The anarchic self wants to oppose totalitarian society through desire and fantasy, but the outcome, as Kundera imagines it, reveals a reality radically different from the one the anarchic self anticipates. The subject of Kundera's fiction is the writer—and in particular the writer's erotic compulsions. In *The Unbearable Lightness of Being* the "epic" obsession, Tomas' womanizing, is an imperative which must be obeyed in much the same way a citizen must submit to a totalitarian regime: *Es muss Sein* (It must be so). The political dimension of Kundera's fiction provides analogies with private life.

Despite the reputed puritanism of totalitarian societies, the erotic life, real or imagined, remains oddly insubordinate.

> He would never command her, as Tomas had, to lay the mirror on the floor and walk back and forth on it naked. Not that he lacks sensuality, he simply lacks the strength to give orders. There are things that can be accomplished only by violence. Physical love is unthinkable without violence.[24]

The irony here is that erotic desire rather than being a force opposed to totalitarian apathy, becomes a new tyranny to which its victims try with dubious success to imagine a counterlife. "Tomas often thought of Tereza's remark about his friend Z and came to the conclusion that the love story of his life exemplified not 'Es muss sein!,'. . . but rather *Es könnte auch anders sein* (It could just as well be otherwise)."[25] These two formulations of Tomas' love story imply two theories of self, narrative, and politics upon which Kundera meditates without committing himself to either. Which is closer to describing Tomas' life? I think the evidence strongly favors *Es muss sein*. The apparent opposition between the erotic and the totalitarian in *The Unbearable Lightness of Being* collapses as the despotic violence of physical love reveals itself. The violence may be directed against the other, but it may also be suffered by the person possessed of erotic desire. A character submits to eros in a way that he or she may not always submit even to a totalitarian regime.

Why should this be? There exists within the desire for an absolute freedom of the self a tyranny of its own making. If we think of the self as a political or social structure in which reason and desire are master class and underclass respectively, then we can envisage the possibility of either class achieving power at the expense of the other to the detriment of the society as a whole: the self. The habit of thinking of the self (the artistic or artistically-inspired self) as an adversary of political and social structures is to divert us from the "political" need of the self to maintain its own structure. In what seems an odd misdirection of energy, the self becomes its own target, in effect shattering itself in the putative interest of its own freedom or, to formulate it somewhat differently, in the interest of greater access to life. It is not as though the shattering of the self is a via media to a new reconstituted self: the very idea of framing, binding, making coherent is under suspicion. The anarchic self has as its target not necessarily the external tyranny of society or the state, but its own impulse toward order. The politics of the anarchic self is based on a misleading analogy between politics and the person, or at the very least on an overdetermined view of the way(s) in which the political and social spheres are internalized in the self.

All effective revolts against tyranny proceed from a counter self-discipline. The risk, of course, is that the discipline that makes the revolution may install itself as a new tyranny; indeed, the risk often becomes reality. But the contrary notion of a liberating anarchy of self and community is an illusion, because the release of new energies occurs at the expense of an emptying of the self. The principled absence of a center from which to act and experience makes the so-called "self" vulnerable to every passion or energy that wishes to assert control. Desire, the essence of life, may become a tyranny. Desire, in *The Unbearable Lightness of Being*, is not the enemy of the state, but a despotism over the self, comparable to the despotism of the state. With the disintegration of a coherent willing subject, eros may be deployed, as Foucault would say, in the interests of any power structure.

It is interesting and, in my view, salutary, that Kundera's imaginative sense of extremity which puts him in the company of postmodern writers is qualified by a classic modernist cautionary wisdom about the difference between writing and living.

> I have known all these situations, I have experienced them myself, yet none of them has given rise to the person my curriculum vitae and I represent. The characters in my novels are my own unrealized possibilities. That is why I am equally fond of them all and equally horrified by them. Each one has crossed a border that I myself have circumvented. It is that crossed border (the border beyond which my own "I" ends) which attracts me most. For beyond that border begins the secret the novel asks about. The novel is not the author's confession; it is an investigation of human life in the trap the world has become.[26]

16

In speaking of the deployment of sexual desire, Foucault brings together the two most formidable terms in contemporary discourse, power and desire. I will discuss Foucault's argument against the Freudian hypothesis of repression in a later chapter, but I want here to express my agreement with Foucault's view that the "essentializing" of sexuality in modern culture, the empowering of it as the primary human energy, has turned sex into tyranny in modern life. One might generalize that the elevating of any human passion or energy at the expense of other passions or energies is an exercise of tyranny. The philosopher Annette Baier has persuasively made the argument against the imperialism of desire.

> We can afford to be pluralists not imperialists in the philosophy of mind, granting an important role to desire without having thereby to banish all its equally vital passion-relatives. Normal people have desires, since they are sensibly concerned with their uncertain futures, and they also have other passions, since not all their hearts' passionate energy is reserved for the uncertain future.[27]

But there remains something troubling in the way Foucault conceives the relation between power and desire. What is curious about contemporary cultural discourse (and Foucault has made an enormous contribution to it) is that as between desire and power, desire is the valued term. It is not sexual desire that is the object of Foucault's critique, but its deployment by institutions of power (the church, the medical establishment). Desire is a word of immense appeal to our sympathies with the oppressed. Power is oppressive and needs to be resisted. Foucault has formulated the influential view that all discourses are power driven and therefore coercive. He is pessimistic about the possibility of a discourse that is free of the power motive, though he believes in the possibility of diffusing it. I would suggest that this formulation is a mystification. We all wish to be empowered and desire is a condition of powerlessness, representing lack or want. Desire is also a sign of vitality, the desiring agent has the power to dream. But desire possesses the subject and signifies incompleteness. How can desire represent authentic being, if it also represents what the self lacks? I think Hannah Arendt was right when she distinguished between power and force: that is, between a power which constitutes and sustains forms of life and violent force that destroys. The effects of power and desire are inversely proportional. For all the celebrations of desire by Dostoevsky's underground man, who identifies desire as life itself, all we see of its operations are the power fantasies of an impotent and resentful man. The underground man's problem is that he is powerless and his cruelty is an expression of powerlessness.

So resentment and desire implicate each other. A desire that aspires toward an illimitable satisfaction and therefore can never be satisfied may become a condition of permanent resentment or, in Max Scheler's words, "an evil secretion in a sealed vessel like prolonged impotence."[28] I would alter the terms of discourse. It is not a case of being for or against desire. What we need to talk about when we talk about desires (plural) are the conditions for their satisfaction. We need to resist the seductive prestige of the word and ask what it means and how it behaves in situations and whether at any particular moment it is worth our devotion. Desires too have their codes, their particular interests and constraints. The desires we value—and even those we disvalue—are unavoidably implicated in morality, reason, convention, that is, all those structures desire in its grand hypostatized incarnation is dedicated to shattering.

I was recently asked by a well-known critic what I was working on. When I told her I was writing a book on desire, she mischievously asked, knowing my tendency toward a certain contrariness, whether I was against desire too. How could I be against desire, it would be like opposing arms, legs, ears and reason? She said she was opposed to reason. Knowing her persuasiveness as a critic, I asked why she then insisted on exercising it. She didn't take what I said as a compliment.

In her contempt for reason and her preference for desire, there lurks the issue of gender—and a paradox. Reason has been associated with the law of the father and patriarchal culture, but so has desire.

> Woman is the most universal and absolute specification of alterity [writes Juliet Mitchell, in glossing Simone de Beauvoir's *The Second Sex*.] No one is born a woman: a woman is created from man's needs.[29]

18

The subject of desire is male, the object female. Freud gave his immense authority to this view when he declared that the libido was masculine. Feminism understandably wants to subvert that claim.

Within another cultural stereotype, however, desire and virility are at odds with each other. Here is Jean-François Lyotard:

> Men (Western men, in any case) want to conquer, not love. They have nothing but disdain and irony for the sensual, for odours, sensations, secretions, *laissez-faire*, music; they call "artists" those among them that consent to these things. But women are the artists. Men feel undone when they love.[30]

Apart from its stereotypical distortion of what actual men are capable of, this limited conception of desire suppresses its willful aspect: desire as the exercise of conquest, in *Heart of Darkness*, for example. Desire is too various and protean to fix in a single incarnation or to attribute to a single gender. I mean to resist these stereotypes. In my account, insofar as possible, desire is gender neutral. I perceive it as a condition assuming many forms, possible to both men and women: in literary terms, to Catherine Earnshaw and Emma Bovary as well as Marcel and Aschenbach. Both men and women may be conceived of as subject or object.

I think it self-defeating to conceive of Reason and Desire as representing ideological choices. First, we need to lower the stakes and reduce them to their lower cases. It is not a matter of deciding between them, but of understanding their complex and changing relationship to each other. The boundaries between reason and desire, like those between writing and living, are neither absolute nor secure. It is neither reasonable nor desirable that they be so. What should not be confused, however, is the idea of the valuable expansion of the boundaries of desire and the self-destructive dream of an existence without boundaries. To choose illimitable desire is to submit oneself to a destructive necessity. To see desires as finite in their ambition is to allow space for the faculty of discrimination and choice.

The erasure of the boundary (any boundary) between reason and desire reflects a modern demystifying discovery that reason may be a mask for desire, interest, or power. Max Weber exposed the instrumental use of reason as the essence of modern bureaucratic life, and Freud revealed the corruptions of rationalization. In my discussion of *Heart of Darkness,* I focus on the ulterior uses of reason for the most monstrously irrational purposes. Like desire, reason is protean (there is more than one kind or use of reason). Certainly rationalization, for example, can hardly be said to exhaust the possibilities of reason. If that were so, Freud's own performance as a demystifier of the rationalizing process would be suspect. To discredit reason because it has been corrupted by rationalization or instrumental uses is to subvert the (rational) process by which one discovers the corruption. If modern life tends to allow an instrumental use of reason to dominate the world, it becomes the task of an ethical criticism and practice to recover and exercise a non-instrumental reason.

There is a view that desire is irresistible, that no effort of mind or will can limit it to boundaries. Jean Baudrillard characterizes as naive and utopian the rationalist claim that "a satisfied need produces a state of equilibrium and resolution of tensions." Baudrillard speaks of an "evanescence and continual mobility [that] reaches a point where it becomes impossible to determine the specific objectivity of needs. . . . The flight from one signifier to another is no more than the surface reality of *a desire,* which is insatiable because it is founded on a lack. And this desire, which can never be satisfied, signifies itself locally in a succession of objects and needs."[31] René Girard has argued that what determines our desire is not its object but our jealous competition for what the other desires. Girard bases his view on love triangles in novels, but the insatiability of mimetic or triangular desire could serve as a model for modern consumerism as well.[32] Illimitable desire may indeed be a tendency of the revolutionary, expansive, and utopian ethos of modern life, an ethos that always promises more than it can deliver. But what is a powerful tendency in modern life need not be construed as an inevitability. In order to distinguish among desires, to be able to decide whether a desire is worth our devotion, we need to reject the homogenizing of desire and entertain the possibility that we can distinguish between natural or genuine desire and artificial or inauthentic desire. We must also not concede the whole psychic space to desire. To do so, we would leave no room for resistance and judgment. Desire becomes the standard of judgment, but it has nothing to judge. My contention is that arguments about the reality of desire and its relationship to reason or morality are at the same time ethical arguments. If, as Hume argues, reason is the slave of desire, why should it be necessary for him to say within the same sentence that it *ought* to be the slave of desire, unless an alternative conception is possible?

How does one arrive at a conception of genuine or natural need in a revolutionary utopian economy, whose business it is to generate (artificial?) desires? One cannot, of course, establish general rules for everyone. Temperaments differ, individuals differ in what they desire. If there is a general principle, it should be that everyone discriminate according to a reflection which leads the person to choose what undestructively satisfies. There will always be a tension between the desires of the self and the impersonal expansive needs of the economy. What is pernicious in the ethos of our advanced economy is its assumption of a vacuous unresistant desiring "nature." Such a view ultimately destroys the integrity and value of the object world. Illimitable desire in its aggressive and perennially discontented consumption of objects becomes —in effect—nihilism. Objects cannot be discriminated and lose all their value. The totalized conception of desire in which objects are irrelevant makes of desire itself a vacuity.

Paradoxically, the effect of conceding the field to illimitable desire is to abort the possibility of satisfaction. The studies of the works of Conrad, Mann, Lawrence, Ford, and Brontë that follow show in greater detail the ambiguously liberating and repressive effects of the imagination of illimitable desire. As we shall see, illimitable desire has many embodiments. It may express itself through the artistic will of Aschenbach in *Death in Venice* or through the erotic will of Birkin in *Women in Love,* or suprisingly and paradoxically through the "rational" will of Kurtz in *Heart of Darkness.*

In characterizing the discourse of desire, I have not felt obliged to demonstrate its total coherence. As in any system of thought, tensions, conflicts, contradictions appear, because the needs it serves cannot always be logically accommodated, though they must be somehow accommodated. Thus desire is at once a vitality, an extravagance and a lack or absence; desire must be distinguished from need, but at times the words may be used interchangeably. It is this inconsistency in the necessary uses of the term that gives it its protean character. One "inconsistency" in my exposition has been my equivocal use of "illimitable desire" as a psychological theme and as an ideological trope. This inconsistency is justified, I believe, by the way the ideology sanctions illimitable desire.

Reason may be an expression of desire (who can deny the insight of the modern tradition?), but it may also work independently of and against desire, without ascetically annihilating it. Desire, I would argue, does not exhaust the possibilities of reason, morality etc. In the essays that follow I deal with fictions in which characters imagine and experience illimitable desire as a tragic truth. I acknowledge the power of this conception (as my elaborate concern with it will make clear), but I do not accept the view that desire need be in its very nature illimitable. By suggesting the possibility of alternatives (the fictions themselves imagine alternatives with varied success), I situate the argument of my book within an ethical discourse. If I fail to provide an *adequate* discussion of alternatives, it is because my polemical purpose is directed against what I understand as a utopian misappropriation of illimitable desire. In order to do so, I need to elicit as fully as possible its tragic implications as well as its imaginative power.

1. ⁊ Conrad's *Heart of Darkness:*
Allegory of Enlightenment

In the introduction, I spoke of the prototypical modernist narrative as enacting unto death the career of desire. *Heart of Darkness* is a very powerful instance of this narrative. Current criticism of *Heart of Darkness* has shifted from a preoccupation with the psychological aspect (often Freudian) to a concern with its political meanings. In the earlier view, the political was seen as an emblem of the psychological. It seems to me that the political and the psychological are intertwined in a way that resists making a hierarchy of their relative importance. Desire plays its part in a political allegory, but politics itself may be read as an enactment of desire.

From the very beginning, Marlow's story connects the themes of conquest and enlightenment. The Romans, agents of an earlier enlightenment, came to conquer England, presumably to civilize it, only to discover a mysterious "wilderness," "a cold fog," "incomprehensible" and ultimately unmasterable. The English wilderness, it would seem, was a place of "utter savagery" that "closed round" the Roman conqueror and consumed him. This, in a phrase, is the conqueror's narrative of defeat. *Heart of Darkness*, I believe, tells a somewhat different story. The savagery is within the conqueror himself, who uses "brute force," and robs and murders in order to gain the objects of desire. The real violence is not in the darkness, but in the action against it, in the "civilized attempt at tackling" the darkness.* Considered in its pristine state, unthreatened and unpenetrated by an alien force, the darkness is a place of "vitality," "intensity," "naturalness," and, yes, "peace."

Readers of the tale have misleadingly associated the darkness with destructive violence. (According to Hillis Miller, for example, "the darkness enters into every gesture of enlightenment to enfeeble it, to hollow it out, to corrupt it and thereby to turn its reason into unreason, its pretense of shedding light into more darkness.")[1] To be sure, the intruder experiences a sense of menace, but Conrad privileges Marlow, also an intruder, with a double-mindedness, an uncanny imagination of what the jungle darkness portends. Thus the natives, who are indistinguishable from the jungle environment, shout, sing, "their eyeballs glistening," their "faces like grotesque masks" and yet Marlow inexplicably finds them "a great comfort to look at." They (and Marlow) seem to belong to "a world of straightforward facts." This feeling passes only when "a man of war anchored off the coast" turns up to "scare it away" incomprehensibly "shelling the bush." Marlow characterizes this behavior as a "touch of insanity," despite the justification "by somebody on board that there was a camp of natives—he called them enemies—hidden out of sight somewhere" (78). The chain gang of black criminals Marlow encounters, displaced from their coastal homes, diseased and dying, is a result of the European invasion, not the expression of innate evil. Nature becomes ominous and destructive only when it perceives the intruder, the alien come to violate it or, perhaps more accurately, when the intruder's perception transforms it.

Every sign of disintegration and death represents a futile trace of the "civilized" will to impose, to dominate, to control: "a

* Joseph Conrad, *Heart of Darkness* (1899) (New York: New American Library, 1950), p. 69. All subsequent references are in the text.

boiler, wallowing in the grass," an overturned "undersized rail-way-truck," "pieces of decaying machinery" (80). The human debris is testimony to the oppressive European will. The chief of the central station speaks of the blacks as transgressors, but it is the Europeans who have transgressed. Marlow will make clear at every turn that the threat of violence does not lie in the outer darkness, but in the will to conquer it.

Marlow does not exempt himself from the judgment. He remembers an earlier time: "I was loafing about, hindering you fellows in your work and invading your homes, just as though I had got a heavenly mission to civilize you" (70). Africa is a blank that he "had a hankering after." And the hankering becomes the most powerful of intellectual weapons, a map that will permit him to penetrate the darkness (71). The river down which he will travel is the deadly snake which will tempt him to violate the prohibition against transgression. Marlow anticipates the appearance of Kurtz not only through the stories he tells, the encounters he has with the accountant, the manager, the harlequin, et al., but in his very presence as an invader of the African continent.

Kurtz is the apotheosis of the Enlightenment will, in the words of "the brickmaker of the Central Station, an emissary of pity and science and progress," a man to be placed in the world "for the guidance of the cause entrusted to us by Europe." Ian Watt persuasively makes the Victorian connection in associating Kurtz with Benthamite Utilitarianism, Social Darwinism, and what he calls "the more spiritual components of the Victorian religion of progress."[2] Without challenging Watt's impressive articulation of Conrad's affinities with English writers and English thought, I have chosen to see *Heart of Darkness* in a more broadly European context (Kurtz, after all, is a Belgian colonizer of German origins) and to view Kurtz's "total Faustian" lack of restraint as a nineteenth-century legacy of the eighteenth-century Enlightenment.

The "central brickmaker," who sees Kurtz as a prodigy of pity, science, and progress, and who attributes to him the guiding power of a "higher intelligence," already anticipates the horror that Kurtz is to experience and embody, when he refers to "the new gang of virtue" that has come on the scene. Kurtz and his gang, the bringers of law, create all the potentialities for transgression. Immediately after the central brickmaker has spoken, Marlow witnesses a scene that unmistakably reflects upon the brick-maker's judgment. He hears a native groaning from a beating he receives at the hands of an "indefatigable" European, who says with satisfaction: "Serve him right. Transgression—punishment—bang! Pitiless, pitiless. That's the only way. This will prevent all conflagrations for the future" (93). The word "transgression" ut-tered by the manager, in isolation, engenders a confusion of refer-ence, however. Who is the transgressor, the black brute, beaten pitilessly by the white law-giver? Or the gang of virtue, invading and conquering the land? "Gang" acquires an unexpected reso-nance.

How to explain the violence of the gang of virtue, the myste-rious workings of the "civilized" will? We are given no clear narrative, only the changing and equivocal view of Marlow: am-biguous, uncertain, enigmatic. What follows is a speculation about the source and nature of the mystery.

Kurtz, Marlow tells us again and again, "lacked restraint in the gratification of his various lusts." This lack of restraint revealed itself through his "magnificent eloquence." "The wilderness had found him out early and had taken on him a terrible vengeance for his fantastic invasion" (133). Here is an invitation to a Freudian reading in which psychic violence would be the return of the repressed, the revolt of the passions against a despotic reason. But in *Heart of Darkness* the will *itself* seems the source of violence, or it is the will that violently redirects energies that in and of them-selves are not violent. In Freudian analysis a partial blame attaches to repressed energies, as though the flaw in the will has been in its failure to respect sufficiently the potential violence of the uncon-scious life. In Conrad, the source of violence is the rational will.

Heart of Darkness confounds the Kantian opposition of reason and desire to which Freud is heir, a dialectic that associates desire with the anarchic, the indeterminate, the insatiable, and reason with control and repression. In Kurtz reason conspires with and magnifies desire. The overwhelming impression made by reason and its corollary virtues of pity and progress is not of limitation and constriction, but of an expansive, unlimited force, set loose upon the world, the very shape of desire itself.

What is the shape of desire? Proust, we have already noted, speaks of desire as unbounded and insatiable: its object forever unattainable. Kurtz's monstrous desires are unspeakable in their horror, but they are also unspeakable in the sense that the objects that define or direct desire are unknown and unattainable: like divinity. The obscurity of language in *Heart of Darkness* reflects the nature of Desire. Desire is the continuous exercise of a will that can never be satisfied. Reason in its valuing of clarity and light may appear to be the antagonist of desire but proves to be its most powerful vehicle. (Progress is an ideal medium for desire. It implies that satisfaction is always in the future, no immediate realization will satisfy.)

Enlightenment reason, as *Heart of Darkness* conceives it, is unrestrained. "Self-consciousness and reason," Herbert Marcuse writes, having "conquered and shaped the historical world, have done so in the image of repression internal and external. They have worked as the agents of domination: the liberties they have brought (and these are considerable) grew in the soil of enslavement and have retained the mark of their birth."[3] In Conrad's version of the career of Enlightenment reason "the image of repression" is external, not internal. The rational will expands to repress the other, not itself. The rational will seeks, but cannot achieve an infinite satisfaction. I doubt whether Enlightenment writers would have viewed their belief in reason as Faustian, though I think the potentiality for this view can be found in their belief in the plasticity of human nature and its capacity for a continuously progressive self-transformation. Reason in the Romantic period is amplified into an instrument of will or desire.

I use the word reason in a specific sense—its expansive hubristic Enlightenment sense. *Heart of Darkness* values reason as restraint and self-limitation; one might even say in its aspect of repression. The novel registers with astonishment the fact that this admirable, modest reason is in the possession of the African natives; indeed, of cannibals who though part of the darkness have in a sense mastered it. The bewildered Marlow declares "Restraint! What possible restraint? Was it superstition, disgust, patience, fear —or some kind of primitive honour? . . . There was the fact facing me" (8). Marlow does not call his restraint "reason," but the implication is, I think, unmistakable. Reason itself is not the culprit in the imperialist drama, but rather the conviction that reason is the unique possession of European civilization, with its hubristic desire to conquer the world. This belief is the poison of racism, a "justification" for bringing civilization to a world that it regards as brutish and irrational. Here Kurtz's national character (his German origins) may be relevant. In an essay called "Autocracy and War," Conrad characterized German nationalism as "a powerful and voracious organization, full of unscrupulous self-confidence, whose appetite for aggrandisement will only be limited by the power of helping itself to the severed members of its friends and neighbors."[4] It would weaken the force of Conrad's tale, however, to see this characteristic as unique to German nationalism. It is an intensified version of a post-Enlightenment European nationalism.

One must in fact distinguish between the "enlightened reason" of Europe and the reason of the cannibals. (I find myself hesitating about whether or where to enclose reason in quotation marks.) European rationalism is based on the notion that the darkness can be overcome. The reason of Africa (and, one might add, Marlow's wisdom) respects the darkness and successfully appeases it. European reason proves to be irrational. Indeed, the jungle exposes the barbarism of the whites and reveals the civility of the Africans. "The reason of Europe" encompasses two versions that are distinguished: the self-interested version in which "reason" is the instrument of a calculated greed, embodied by the Eldorado Expedition, and the disinterested version, the rational-ethical idea that apparently motivates Kurtz's expedition.[5] The profundity of *Heart of Darkness* lies in its perception of what underlies the disinterested version: a *desire* for power so extreme and so immense as to render the greed of the Eldorado buccaneers trivial by comparison. This is not a simple matter of demystification, the discovery of a mean economic reality under the veil of an apparent idealism. It is rather the exposure of the anatomy of Western idealism itself: the desire of a reason that does not know itself to conquer a world that cannot be conquered.

Kurtz has discovered the hollowness at the center of the enlightened European being. I am careful to characterize his discovery in this way, because his hollowness must not be confused with the darkness external to him, a darkness that remains palpable and substantial throughout the tale. (The hollowness may be read as *lack* which, as we have already understood, is an essential aspect of most conceptions of desire.) Kurtz's hubris consists precisely in his failure to honor the darkness. To say that emptiness is the pervasive condition of the world is to globalize the hollowness of the European soul.

Have I overstated the case for the ferocity of the civilized will and the relative benignity of the wilderness? The Conradian wilderness is no romantic idyll; it is a place of sorrow, savagery, disease, and death, "a land of darkness and sorrow," in the phrase of the narrator of "An Outpost of Progress," a tale that exhibits remarkable affinities with *Heart of Darkness.*[6] But it also contains a powerful and splendid life, of which the European intelligence, dependent on the "high organization [and safety] of civilized crowds," is stupidly oblivious. In "An Outpost of Progress" Conrad represents discursively what is mystifyingly dramatized in *Heart of Darkness:*

> They lived like blind men in a large room, aware only of what came in contact with them (and of that imperfectly), but unable to see the general aspect of things. The river, the forest, all the great land throbbing with life, were like a great emptiness. Even the brilliant sunshine disclosed nothing intelligible. Things appeared and disappeared before their eyes in an unconnected and aimless kind of way. The river seemed to come from nowhere and flow nowhither. It flowed through a void. . . .[7]

This moment of incomprehension interests Conrad, as does the contrast between European blindness, evidenced by the fear and the violence it creates, and the life of the wilderness (which he shows to its best advantage).

The Enlightenment was a great age of demystification. Its project was to bring light where there was darkness, truth where there was falsity. The effect of Kurtz's adventure is to expose the presumption of the demystifier, to reveal the ultimacy of darkness. If it weren't for the misleading character of the images evoked, one might say that *Heart of Darkness* demystifies demystification. Kurtz's nihilism (his descent into the abyss) confirms the value of "the surface truths" that occupy Marlow's existence. It endorses the kind of story that Marlow tells, "the meaning . . . enveloping the tale." Marlow returns from his meeting with Kurtz, empowered to tell his story, because of his capacity to bear witness to what he is incapable of enacting.

Europe and Africa: Conrad does not simply invert the hierarchy. He destroys it through establishing a bond between the cannibals and Marlow. Conrad's "technique" has its basis in the psychological phenomenon that Freud analyses in his essay "On the Uncanny." Marlow discovers the affinity of his own mind with the dark life of the jungle.

> The earth seemed unearthly. We are accustomed to look upon the shackled form of a conquered monster, but there—there you could look at a thing monstrous and free. It was unearthly, and the men were. . . . No, they were not inhuman. Well, you know, that was the worst of it—this suspicion of their not being inhuman. It would come slowly to one. They howled and leaped, and spun, and made horrid faces; but what thrilled you was just the thought of their humanity—like yours—the thought of your remote kinship with this wild and passionate uproar. Ugly. Yes, it was ugly enough; but if you were man enough you would admit to yourself that there was in you just the faintest trace of a response to the terrible frankness of that noise, a dim suspicion of there being a meaning in it which you —you so remote from the night of first ages—could comprehend. And why not? The mind of man is capable of anything— because everything is in it, all the past as well as all the future. (105–6)

Freud characterizes the "uncanny [as] in reality nothing new or alien, but something which is familiar and old—established in the mind and has become alienated from it only through the process of repression."[8]

But it is not only the dark side that establishes an affinity between Marlow and the African natives. They share a modest commitment to the will. Their aim is not mastery of others, but self-possession. The rivets that Marlow desires for his disintegrating boat, the instructions in Towson's manual belong to his work ethic. The final portrait that emerges of Marlow is of a Buddha-like self-mastery that flows out into the unthreatening darkness of the universe. Marlow has in effect been divested of his European character: it is the human bond with the Africans not the difference from them that matters.

There is an affinity between *Heart of Darkness* and the theoretical work of Theodor Adorno and Max Horkheimer of the Frankfurt School, in particular *Dialectic of Enlightenment*. For

Adorno and Horkheimer, Enlightenment reason is inauthentic and untrue. In attempting to dominate nature and himself, man destroys himself. "Man's domination over himself, which grounds his selfhood, is almost always the destruction of the subject in whose service it is undertaken."[9] The sentence could stand as a motto for Kurtz's adventure. As could the following sentences stand for the significance of Kurtz's unequaled eloquence. "Speech, though it deludes physical force, is incapable of restraint . . . the word knows that it is weaker than the nature that it has deceived. Too much talking allows force and injustice to prevail as the actual principle, and therefore prompts those who are to be feared always to commit the very action that is feared."[10] Speech "liberates" what is repressed. What is repressed turns out to be the most coercive, the most repressive energies. The unconscious compels speech (a version of writing) and speech compels others. If speech is coercive, what is the status of *Heart of Darkness,* which has few rivals for sheer loquacity? Speech occupies most of the writing of *Heart of Darkness,* and it comes to us from Marlow rather than Kurtz. It tries to express the unsayable, that is, the region of the unconscious.

Adorno and Horkheimer do not choose irrationalism as an alternative to Enlightenment reason; rather they seek dialectically to transcend an inauthentic reason and achieve a reason that harmonizes with nature. Their philosophy depends upon a distinction first made by Max Weber between reason as an end and reason as a means or instrument. Enlightenment reason, in Weber's view, had been reduced to an instrumentality. Accepting Weber's diagnosis, Adorno and Horkheimer envisioned a redemption of reason through its reconciliation with nature; that is, its relinquishment of the project of domination. If Conrad remains committed to reason, it is to the modest stoic version embodied in Marlow, in the cannibals, who have "learned" to live and work on the surface of existence.

Adorno and Horkheimer propose a radical critique of the Enlightenment in which a reason more responsive to nature and desire transcends the repressive reason of the Enlightenment. But this new reason is as of yet inchoate and provokes the suspicion that it will be another "repressive" reason with its rules and its exclusions as well as its inclusions. Conrad, however, has no utopian theoretical position. He remains very much the rationalist whose commitment to reason is commonsensical and "conservative." The Victorian work ethic suggests an Aristotelian ideal of active moderation, remote from a hypostasized reason that may be the flip side of essential desire.

My reading of *Heart of Darkness* is clearly at odds with the revisionist view, most forcefully articulated by the Nigerian novelist Chinua Achebe, that *Heart of Darkness* is a racist tale that "projects the image of Africa as 'the other world,' the antithesis of Europe and therefore of civilization where man's vaunted intelligence and refinement are finally mocked by triumphant bestiality."[11] The revisionist argument rests largely on the white and black, light and dark dichotomies that characterize the tale. Benita Parry acknowledges Conrad's effort to subvert them, but then quite arbitrarily asserts that "black and dark do serve the text as equivalences for the savage and unredeemed, the corrupt and degraded. . . . Imperialism itself is perceived as the dark within Europe . . . the fiction gravitates back to established practice, registering the view of two incompatible orders within a Manichean universe."[12] But Conrad does succeed in subverting the dichotomies. Nothing is more lurid in *Heart of Darkness* than the whited sepulchral city, the morbid pallor of Kurtz's Intended or, for that matter, the ivory which is the object of European greed. Nothing is more consoling than the vital energies of the dark wilderness. Marlow's tale, as the peripheral narrator notes, is precisely a narrative of blurring in which the opposition of light and dark cannot be sustained.

> The yarns of seamen have a direct simplicity, the whole meaning of which lies within the shell of a cracked nut. But Marlow was not typical (if his propensity to spin yarns be excepted), and to him the meaning of an episode was not inside like a kernel but outside, enveloping the tale which brought it out only as a glow brings out a haze, in the likeness of one of these misty halos that sometimes are made visible by the spectral illumination of moonshine. (68)

Light does not have the authority of clarity or truth. Marlow's manner is that of a counter-Enlightenment fable. The corruptive force in *Heart of Darkness* is not darkness, but an illimitable reason, "imaged" as light itself, the mask of desire, what Nietzsche calls the will to power. It is hard to resist the feeling that it is Conrad's critics who are possessed by the conventional stereotypes and simply fail to recognize a subversion when they see one. Parry and other critics *assume* that the white-black, light-dark dichotomies have their origins in white racism. (I should note here an apparent inconsistency in my argument which, I think, represents an inconsistency or perhaps a double strategy in Conrad himself: in order to subvert the Enlightenment claim, Conrad or Marlow will either invert the light-dark opposition or confound it.)

It is difficult to deal with the complaint that Conrad's perspective is Eurocentric. What else could it be? The issue is whether he justifies or criticizes the European perspective. Conrad does not have an anthropological understanding of African cultures. He neither assumes the existence of an African culture nor (it would follow) does he imagine the African perspective from within. If he assumed an African culture, however, it does not follow he would be able to imagine that culture from within. How could he?

And yet I cannot rest content with a reading of *Heart of Darkness* as a cautionary tale about the horrors of the European will in the nineteenth century. Such a reading leaves out of account Marlow's ambivalence toward Kurtz, his extraordinary admiration of him, despite what he knows about him. Indeed, the progress of the narrative goes from, what we might expect of the sober-minded Marlow, an unillusioned view of Kurtz (he begins by mistrusting everything he hears about Kurtz) to a surprising enchantment with this "gifted creature" and "his ability to talk, his words—the gift of expression, the bewildering, the illuminating, the most exalted and the most contemptible, the pulsating stream of light, or the deceitful flow from the heart of an impenetrable darkness" (119–20). Marlow's enchantment becomes a coercive eloquence representing Kurtz, whose reputed eloquence we never directly hear; it confounds the exalted and the contemptible, the light and the darkness. It is as if Marlow, like John the Baptist, prepares us for an encounter with someone who transcends him.

Yet what is it that the transcendent Kurtz embodies but the ideology of the cruelest imperialism that Europe has ever known, the Belgian conquest of the Congo? Marlow notes "the argument" with an "enthusiasm" that makes him "tingle." He quotes Kurtz: "We whites, from the point of development we had arrived at,

must necessarily appear to them [savages] in the nature of supernatural being—we approach them with the might as of a deity!"
(123). And he goes on to speak of Kurtz's "peroration" as "magnificent," giving him "the notion of an exotic Immensity ruled by
an august Benevolence." Marlow, to be sure, speaks of his enthusiasm in retrospect, "The opening paragraph strikes me now as
ominous." Nor does he fail to note the perverse logic of the
"august Benevolence. . . . Exterminate all the brutes." One might
think that Marlow is exercising a forceful irony here. But no, he
will make clear his complicity in suppressing this piece of benevolence in order to protect Kurtz's reputation, as he does in the lie
he tells to Kurtz's bride. Marlow's motive in telling the lie (he says
the last word that Kurtz uttered was her name) is usually understood as compassionate consideration for her, a reflection of the
realization that she would not survive the knowledge of what
Kurtz had become. But Marlow's humane circumspection hardly
explains his deep and tenacious loyalty to Kurtz, his willingness to
be Kurtz's messenger to the world.

The crucial passage involves an extended comparison or rather
contrast between Marlow and Kurtz, and at Marlow's expense. It
concerns the confrontation with the abyss and death: the terms of
our understanding of Kurtz go beyond politics to metaphysics. It
is a long and powerful passage in which Marlow distinguishes his
own "unexciting" and unheroic wrestling with death from Kurtz's
heroic plunge into the abyss.

> I have wrestled with death. It is the most unexciting contest you
> can imagine. It takes place in an impalpable greyness, with noth-
> ing underfoot, with nothing around, without spectators, without
> clamour, without glory, without the great desire of victory,
> without the great fear of defeat, in a sickly atmosphere of tepid
> scepticism, without much belief in your own right, and still less
> in that of your adversary. If such is the form of ultimate wisdom,
> then life is a greater riddle than some of us think it to be. I was
> within a hair's breadth of the last opportunity for pronounce-
> ment, and I found with humiliation that probably I would have
> nothing to say. This is the reason why I affirm that Kurtz was a
> remarkable man. He had something to say. He said it. Since I
> had peeped over the edge myself, I understand better the mean-
> ing of his stare, that could not see the flame of the candle, but
> was wide enough to embrace the whole universe, piercing enough

to penetrate all the hearts that beat in the darkness. He had summed up—he had judged. "The horror!" He had made that last stride, he had stepped over the edge, while I had been permitted to draw back my hesitating foot. And perhaps in this is the whole difference; perhaps all the wisdom, and all truth, and all sincerity, are just compressed into that inappreciable moment of time in which we step over the threshold of the invisible. (148–49)

Commentators have struggled with dubious success to articulate the "something" that Kurtz had to say. Certainly "the horror, the horror" is insufficient both in eloquence and reference to constitute in itself the "summing up" that Marlow believes Kurtz to have achieved. If anyone in *Heart of Darkness* seems to have something to say, it is Marlow, and yet he states without equivocation (and with no evidence of false modesty) "probably I would have nothing to say." One might explain the paradox perhaps as Marlow's dependence on Kurtz for whatever articulateness he has achieved. Marlow in effect assumes the role of Kurtz's alter ego. But the question remains: What does Kurtz/Marlow have to say?

Kurtz achieves an experience that Marlow can represent in the language of action, which makes Kurtz at once singular and exemplary. First there is "the stare . . . wide enough to embrace the whole universe, piercing enough to penetrate all the hearts that beat in the darkness." Then there is "the last stride, he had stepped over the edge." What seems to compel Marlow's admiration is precisely and perversely what makes for the horror, Kurtz's unbridled will—his desire for mastery of the world, a desire which leads to death. Power, mastery, authority: they are the irresistible objects of admiration and fascination, despite what one knows of the horrible costs, despite the fact that they may lead to their opposite, destruction and death. The desire for mastery and power results in destruction when it is not based on self-knowledge and self-mastery. If Marlow survives the apocalyptic debacle at the end it is because he has come to know himself, that is, to know his limits. But clearly such self-knowledge and self-mastery are not enough: the imagination longs to surpass the ethical in order to achieve a nihilist truth. The issues of mastery and authority remain unresolved in *Heart of Darkness*. It would be instructive, I think, to look elsewhere in Conrad for a resolution. I have in mind *The*

Secret Sharer, another short work of fiction, composed years later, with which *Heart of Darkness* has often been coupled.

The Secret Sharer is a story about the mystery of personhood. The plot is relatively simple: the narrator has just been made captain of a ship, his first command and through several small actions at the beginning of the story exhibits insecurity. Through his oversight a ladder is left hanging over the side of the ship and a man suddenly appears, the escaped chief mate from another ship who, in a fit of indignant passion, had murdered a mutinous sailor. The remainder of the tale consists of intimate and defensive transactions between the captain and Leggatt, his uninvited visitor. Surprisingly, the captain treats him as more than a guest, "a secret sharer" he calls him, and protects him against discovery by the crew and Leggatt's own captain, who seeks him out for punishment. In the end Leggatt is given a dubious kind of freedom. At the moment that the captain speaks of his newly gained sense of mastery and authority ("the perfect communion of a seaman with his first command"), Leggatt, the fugitive, is released into the sea and is somewhat mystifyingly perceived as "a free man, a proud swimmer striking out for a new destiny."*

As it unfolds, the tale introduces a series of puzzles, the solutions of which contribute to the solution of the mystery. Why does Leggatt suddenly appear to the captain as a headless corpse? What is the significance of the circumstances of Leggatt's appearance? What attracts the captain to Leggatt? Why does he conceal him and fail to turn him over to the authorities? Is the concealment of Leggatt plausible or does it compromise the realistic decorum of the tale? Is the story hallucinatory or realistic? These are very precise questions and they demand precise answers. The tale unfolds with a rigorous narrative logic that generates questions and answers, which will solve the mystery with which it begins. I view the inexorable logic of the story as a problem, if not a flaw, which I will later address, but it is important to see it as essential to the story.

The questions that I have posed above depend for their answers on the prior question about the captain himself and how he sees himself. He speaks of being "a stranger to himself," divided

---

* *The Secret Sharer* (1910) (New York: Signet, 1971), p. 19. All subsequent references are in the body of the text.

between his actual self and an ideal conception of himself, a division that is the source of his insecurity and uncertainty about his authority. "I wondered how far I should turn out faithful to that ideal conception of one's own personality every man sets up for himself secretly" (21). The ideal conception of himself is not defined, but it soon becomes clear that it implicates the *authority* that he has in name only. It involves the mastery of the ship, a precondition to which is mastery of himself. What is of crucial interest to us is that the self is *given* as internally divided. The self-unity and authority the captain achieves is the result of a profound psychological transaction between him and his secret sharer.

I think it can be demonstrated that every event in the story, even its accidents, belongs to a chain of psychological necessity. Every external event is triggered by a psychological condition of the captain. For example, the presence of the rope ladder that made it possible for Leggatt to climb aboard was the result of the captain's insecurity, which led him to dismiss all hands without setting an anchor watch. The captain feels threatened by the critical scrutiny of his chief mate and dismisses him and the rest of the crew. He wants to prove his authority by taking command, and in the process displays a lack of authority which involves the capacity to delegate it. This episode is not an "accident," but a link in a chain of psychological necessity. The plot of *The Secret Sharer* is closely linked to the captain's state of mind, his desires and fears.

The Secret Sharer implicitly attributes to the narrative act powers of self-realization and transformation. Leggatt's power lies in his capacity as storyteller; the captain's "salvation" in his own capacity to absorb and internalize the story—to make it his own. By living out imaginatively the violence Leggatt commits—and it is important to emphasize living it out through an agent whose values are perceived to be his own (they have gone to the same school)—the captain is able to exorcise the demons of violence, the source of his insecurity, in his own soul. The act of exorcism would not occur if the captain were merely a passive auditor of Leggatt's tale. While the captain listens he acts out the most strenuous intrigue of concealment and protection of Leggatt. Through the complicity with his secret sharer, the captain undergoes an ordeal that enables him to achieve self-confidence and authority. It is almost as if the captain is telling himself his own story. The captain imagines what an observer would see if he were present: "as we stood leaning over my bed place, whispering side by side, with our dark heads together and our backs to the door, anybody bold enough to open it stealthily would have been treated to the uncanny sight of a double captain busy talking in whispers with his other self" (31). The exorcism of our captain's personal demons is marked by the return of Leggatt to the sea.

> And I was alone with her. Nothing! no one in the world should stand now between us, throwing a shadow on the way of silent knowledge and mute affection, the perfect communion of a seaman with his first command. (61)

The captain's newly acquired sense of unity and "perfect communion" with his first command depends upon his separation from Leggatt, whose role as double has (necessarily) exacerbated the sense of alienation from self and ship that plagued the captain from the very beginning of the story.

The moment of release is a moment of crisis. In bringing the ship close to shore so that Leggatt can swim to safety, the captain risks shipwreck but at the same time avoids it through the agency of Leggatt whose hat, cast by him upon the waters, serves as a marker. The moment registers with particular force the ambiguous role that Leggatt plays throughout the story: he is at once danger and salvation. And it registers another aspect of Leggatt's role: an autonomy that makes him indeed the captain's double. That is, Leggatt does not function merely as the dark and violent side of the captain's being—the murderous impulses of unconscious life. He is a fully developed and complex character, who like the captain and indeed before him has achieved control over his impulses, though unlike the captain he committed a murder. Leggatt embodies not only the potentiality for violence in the captain, indeed in everyone, he has actualized the violence and passed on to self-possession and a kind of freedom. Leggatt is the *bouc emmisaire*, the scapegoat, the martyr, who shows others the way.

The question remains: how consistent is the narrative logic of *The Secret Sharer* and what does it signify? The note of closure (the perfect communion) is too absolute. The conflicts that the story describes like the conflicts in the Freudian dualisms are too powerful and enduring for any permanent resolution. Yet the resolution has about it an air of finality, not even a shadow between the captain and his ship. The narrative logic is overdetermined by the psychological need of the captain—and we may surmise of the author himself. One might argue that this is a fiction of the self in which the author is overcommitted to the ideal of authority.

Narrative is a form of writing that represents a double movement at once centrifugal and centripetal. Narrative implies that the subject is not unitary or that its unity is illusory or unstable. Narrative unfolds, reveals the variety of the subject (one possible definition of plot) in which the event or episode of the external world is the catalyst. In Freudian terms, narrative is the continual displacement of the subject, its capacity for self-revelation and coherence. Desire is the motive, the moving spirit of narrative, because it represents what the self lacks or wants. Its telos, never to be truly realized, is what would complete the self. Writing acts out the desire (unconscious or hidden) of the subject. Its aim is self-completion, i.e., closure. But if desire is in its very nature insatiable, meaning that the subject is always wanting, then closure becomes an arbitrary resolution: it remains a permanently elusive object of desire. Here we have the reason why all narrative closures become suspect. The modernist solution is for the ending to suggest openness, ambiguity. Narrative in its deviousness, its deferral of satisfaction, its discovery of satisfaction in deferral is a reproach to all premature claims to unity and wholeness. Desire keeps the subject open. It needs to be stressed, however, that even if closure is illusory, a will-o'-the-wisp, the drive toward closure, i.e., coherence is incorrigible: it is the essence of narrative.

Narrative in *The Secret Sharer* is constructed as a causal chain, harnessing all the countervailing energies. The captain's vulnerable psyche does *not* open up to the energies that might overthrow it, but is rather put into the service of a logic at once psychological and narrative that will ineluctably integrate and strengthen it. For instance, even Leggatt's violent act is moralized: he lost control by trying to constrain a mutinous mate at a moment of crisis at sea. What is a pre-moral unconscious in Freud is completely moralized and rationalized in the Conradian equivalent in *The Secret Sharer*.

Freud's essay on the uncanny, written without the benefit of a reading of Conrad, illuminates *The Secret Sharer*. Freud defines "the double" as the product of "a special agency [in the psyche] which is able to stand over against the rest of the ego, which has the function of observing and criticizing the self and of exercising a censorship within the mind, and which we become aware of as our 'conscience.' "[13] In a footnote, Freud expresses the belief that "when popular psychologists talk of the splitting of people's egos, what they are thinking of is this division (in the sphere of ego psychology) between the critical agency and the rest of the ego, and not the antithesis discovered by psychoanalysis between the ego and what is unconscious and repressed. It is true that the distinction between these two antitheses is to some extent effaced by the circumstance that foremost among the things that are rejected by the criticism of the ego are derivatives of the repressed."[14] This is about as succinct an account as one might wish of the dual function of Leggatt, who represents at once or on different occasions the repressed energies of violence latent in the captain and the critical agency of conscience, the superego. In Freud's view the superego has its genesis "as a representative of the id and of its derivatives, and [he] ascribes much of its harshness, severity and inexorability" to its origins.[15] Violence in *The Secret Sharer* does not have its source in a dark inchoate Freudian id, but in authority itself.

But authority is not an ultimate explanation of the violence on the Sephora, the mutinous act, nor Leggatt's murderous response. What motivates both violence and authority is fear, which the narrator of "An Outpost of Progress" characterizes as the deepest and most tenacious human emotion: "Fear always remains. A man may destroy everything within himself, love and hate and belief, and even doubt; but as long as he clings to life he cannot destroy fear; the fear, subtle, indestructible, and terrible, that pervades his being; that tinges his thoughts; that lurks in his heart; that watches on his lips the struggle of his last breath."[16] Fear is inextricably bound up with the instinct for survival. It turns to violence when the self feels threatened. It takes on the mask of authority to protect itself against the other. Fear is an inescapable emotion, contemptible only when it overwhelms a life. The man of fear is a coward, but the repression of fear in a fantasy of absolute control or power can dehumanize the soul.

In *Heart of Darkness* Conrad had imagined a necessitous darkness that threatened the narrative structure itself. *The Secret Sharer* has little of the indeterminacy of language, uncertainty of reference and hesitation about meaning and significance that we find in *Heart of Darkness*. In *The Secret Sharer* narrative reasserts itself in its causal organization and its symbolic certainties in the interests of mastery.

If we adopt a Freudian perspective, what we see is a masculine world dominated exclusively by a desire for authority over self and world in which Eros is totally absent. It is a world ruled by Thanatos. In *Civilization and Its Discontents* Freud postulates Eros and Thanatos as mythical figures that represent the eternal conflict between the sexual and the aggressive (life destructive) instincts. Though Freud's view of that conflict is Manichean (neither Eros nor Thanatos will ultimately triumph), Freud imagines the possibility of provisional redemptions of the destructive work of Thanatos by Eros. But Conrad imagines no such redemptions, or at least he does not in *The Secret Sharer*. The aggressive instincts are mastered and contained by a counter aggression: the aggression of authority. I would argue that *The Secret Sharer* affirms Leggatt's violence, because it is on behalf of authority. If the tale has a villain, it is the captain of the Sephora, whose blind devotion to the law reflects weakness rather than strength. That is, the captain does not appreciate what Leggatt (whose name conjures up "legality") profoundly understands: that violence, sometimes extreme violence, is required to uphold the law. Conrad's characters are possessed of the violence of Thanatos, which in its defense of authority may destroy life. Paradoxically, the containment of violence in the interests of self-mastery may produce a stoic imperviousness that suggests the renunciation of life.

In *Heart of Darkness,* Conrad dramatizes the provisional nature of all so-called civilized attempts to master the darkness. In *The Secret Sharer,* I discern, in the light of the knowledge that Conrad presumably achieved in the earlier work, an inordinate impulse toward and belief in the possibility of mastery. Marlow's ambivalent admiration for Kurtz is here resolved. No shadow falls on the masterful will, the dream of rational control over others as well as oneself is realized. All that is required is a displacement of the possibility of violence to a scapegoat, who is sent away never to return.

However problematic the "solution" of *The Secret Sharer* may be, it represents a significant counterimage to the temptation of illimitable desire. It affirms self-knowledge, the knowledge of one's limits as the pre-condition for the constructive exercise of power. Mastery of the world presupposes self-mastery, a condition that eluded Kurtz. Marlow achieves self-mastery but only for the sake of self-possession. His being in the world is unworldly, Buddha-like and contributes to the dominant impression of apocalyptic despair. In *The Secret Sharer*, Conrad tried to imagine the conditions of a constructive and humane exercise of worldly power. *The Secret Sharer* fails to be convincing because it does not acknowledge as does *Heart of Darkness* the immensity of the ungovernable power unleashed by illimitable desire. It finesses the challenge through narrative strategy.

Together *Heart of Darkness* and *The Secret Sharer* testify to the paradoxical relationship of the Enlightenment to the life of reason. For all its vaunting of reason, the Enlightenment contributed to the overthrow of ethical reason, cultivated so strenuously by the Socratic tradition, by reconceiving reason as an instrument of the will to power without presupposing self-mastery through the knowledge of limits.

Where does this place Conrad on the political spectrum? The desire for mastery (in its Enlightenment version) is a revolutionary desire. It wants to overturn and reorder the world. The desire for mastery may also come from a conservative impulse to maintain order. What distinguishes these two desires is the difference between expansiveness and constriction, between aggrandizement and repression. I think Conrad in *Heart of Darkness*, to the extent that he is a critic of the will, is a critic of it in its revolutionary and imperial forms. The historical prototype for the revolutionary and imperial will is Napoleon. (*Kurz*, we should remember, means "short" in German.) Where Conrad is complicit with the desire for mastery (as in the *The Secret Sharer*), it tends to be in its conservative form. By "conservative," I do not mean reactionary, nor do I mean the particular political tendencies that designate themselves as conservative in Western society. Conservative signifies the will to preserve structures (like the structure of a ship). It may even conspire with progressive tendencies (like the building of a railroad). It recoils from the violent will, though it has its own fear-driven capacity for violence.

42

But the difference, the respectability of Conrad's version of authority should not divert us from what both versions have in common, a desire for mastery and authority over self and world, which may be a life instinct, deeper than the ideological versions that are in conflict with each other. We may need to keep this fact in mind (and I believe it to be a fact) at a time when a perspective (often but not always associated with Foucault) has gained authority in the academy which disparages the very idea of power at the same time that it acknowledges its inevitability. The issue is not whether power itself is a good or an evil (everyone wishes to be empowered), but how its exercise can be made humane.

2 ?❀ The Art of Ambivalence: Mann's *Death in Venice*

Desire seeks to possess and command an object that forever eludes it. Power, it would seem, is the object of desire. *Death in Venice* begins with its hero in power. He is the master artist of his time, whose career is "attended by the applause and adulation of the masses."* His artistic stature gives him political and social authority: his books become the classroom texts that will help form the mind of the nation. *Death in Venice* is a story about the disintegration of *this* power under the pressure of desire. The object of desire turns out to be more elusive and more awesome than Aschenbach's extraordinary success. The irony is that success depends upon imagination, whose source is desire, the very vehicle of his subsequent undoing.

* Thomas Mann, *Death in Venice and Seven Other Stories* (1911), translated by H. T. Lowe Porter (New York: Vintage, 1954–1962), p. 14. All subsequent references are in the text.

The portrait of Aschenbach is of a particular kind of artist, one of will rather than inspiration ("he had never known the careless freedom of youth"). The qualities of will are given to us in such phrases as "a clenching of the teeth," "self-command," "sheer self-abnegation," "labouring at the edge of exhaustion," "skillful husbanding" and "prodigious spasms of will." The ambition of the author of the life of Frederick of Prussia, *Maia,* and *The Abject* is to show that a man "can still be capable of moral resolution even after he has plumbed the depths of knowledge" (8).

Aschenbach's moral conscience is not a matter of choice. Mann makes unmistakably clear that it is the result of a legacy, a sort of genetic endowment. "His forbears had been officers, magistrates, government functionaries, men who had led severe, steady lives serving their king, their state" (12). So it is fitting that Aschenbach's books become classics:

> With time, an official note, something almost expository, crept into Gustave Aschenbach's method. His later style gave up the old sheer audacities, the fresh and subtle nuances—it became fixed and exemplary, conservative, formal, even formulated. Like Louis XIV—or as tradition has it of him—Aschenbach, as he went on in years, banished from his style every common word. It was at this time that the school authorities adopted selections from his works into their textbooks. And he found it only fitting —and had no thought but to accept—when a German prince signalized his accession to the throne by conferring upon the poet-author of the life of Frederick the Great on his fiftieth birthday the letters-patent of nobility. (14)

Aschenbach's is an art of containment or repression of desire. Louis XIV and Frederick are political exemplars of mastery, counterparts to his own position as artist. He is the masterful bourgeois artist whose formalist art expresses or perhaps legislates the stabilities of bourgeois society.

From the perspective of the traditional bourgeois-bohemian opposition, the phrase "bourgeois artist" is oxymoronic. The figure of the artist since the Romantic period has been the anarchic anti-bourgeois bohemian possessed by demons, pursuing beauty at the expense of conventional morality. At the same time art, which has its own conventions, makes formal demands upon the artist. An anarchist in society, the artist might be a formalist, a creature of conventions in his art. The formal and disciplinary aspect of art shares the repressiveness of the bourgeois structure. Early on, the narrator characterizes the ambiguity that anticipates the main dramatic tension of the tale.

> And has not form two aspects? Is it not moral and immoral at once: moral insofar as it is the expression and result of discipline, immoral—yes, actually hostile to morality—in that of its very essence it is indifferent to good and evil, and deliberately concerned to make the moral world stoop beneath its proud and undivided sceptre? (13)

Aschenbach's self-command proves to be a futile effort to resolve the ambiguity by imposing the discipline of form. The instability of the discipline registers itself in the restlessness that impels Aschenbach to go on holiday. Aschenbach's choice of Venice, made after an abortive decision to go to Trieste ("the society at the hotel was provincial, Austrian, and limited, too much like the life he was trying to get away from") *seems* absolutely right, inevitable when he makes it: "the incomparable, the fabulous, the like-nothing-else-in-the-world" (16). Venice represents the possibility of escape from the burdens and austerities of art, which have left him, at the age of fifty, exhausted. In temporarily abandoning his work as an artist, as the maker of beautiful form, he chooses a city that he sees as the very incarnation of beauty. The escape from the workaday world of art will prove illusory.

The main event of Aschenbach's journey turns out to be his encounter with Tadzio. And he responds to Tadzio as he does to Venice. Like Venice, Tadzio is a work of art. "The lad's perfect beauty" evokes in Aschenbach's mind "the noblest monument of Greek sculpture" (25). But Tadzio's perfection is only one side of the story. The ethical ambiguity of art is exemplified in the description of Tadzio (through the eyes of Aschenbach). The boy at once embodies "a *chaste* perfection of form" and "a *wanton* and treacherous proneness to break hearts" (26). As it turns out, Venice is not an escape from art but a discovery of its deepest impulses. His version of the Phaedrus myth represents the logic of the destructive complicity between art and desire.

> For mark you, Phaedrus, beauty alone is both divine and visible; and so it is the sense way, the artist's way, little Phae-

drus, to the spirit. But, now tell me, my dear boy, do you believe that such a man can ever attain wisdom and true manly worth, for whom the path to the spirit must lead through the senses? Or do you rather think—for I leave the point to you—that it is a path of perilous sweetness, a way of transgression, and must surely lead him who walks in it astray? . . . But detachment, Phaedrus, and preoccupation with form lead to intoxication and desire, they may lead the noblest among us to frightful emotional excesses, which his own stern cult of the beautiful would make him the first to condemn. So they too, they too, lead to the bottomless pit. (72–73)

The preoccupation with beautiful form leads to intoxication, stimulates desire and causes frightful emotional excess. The path to the abyss is inevitable, because beautiful form cannot free itself from its sensuous aspect, and the senses are the route to the passions. Art inevitably betrays its commitment to form and reveals its true identity as an enemy of the bourgeois order, indeed of all order, including that which constitutes the health of the body. In Nietzschean terms, the artist's "progress" is from an Apollonian to a Dionysian conception of art, which entails self-destruction as reflected in Aschenbach's dream of the "Stranger God."

But now the dreamer was in them and of them, the stranger god was his own. Yes, it was he who was flinging himself upon the animals, who bit and tore and swallowed smoking gobbets of flesh—while on the trampled moss there now began the rites in honour of the god, an orgy of promiscuous embraces—and in his very soul he tasted the bestial degradation of his fall. (66–68)

Aschenbach's public career as artist represents an attempt to make art an institution of civilization, and like other institutions an instrument of order. In *Civilization and Its Discontents* Freud argues that all exercises of repression (the more severe they become) provoke the return of the repressed. The effect of a severe aesthetic formalism can be brought into this understanding. But *Death in Venice* implies the exceptional character of aesthetic formalism (of the preoccupation with beautiful form), for however strong its conscious commitment to a doctrine of control, the very preoccupation with beauty makes for a complicity with sensuous and passional energies which it tries to contain.

As with *Heart of Darkness,* Mann's tale cannot be reduced simply to its psychological categories. Indeed, political, psychological, moral, social, and aesthetic categories are virtually interchangeable. Consider the following meditation on the plague that besets Venice (a collaborative effort of Aschenbach and the narrator?):

> And he felt in his heart a curious elation at these events impending in the world about him. Passion is like crime: it does not thrive on the established order and the common round; it welcomes every blow dealt the bourgeois structure, every weakening of the social fabric, because therein it feels a sure hope of its own advantage. These things that were going on in the unclean alleys of Venice, under cover of an official hushing-up policy—they gave Aschenbach a dark satisfaction. The city's evil secret mingled with the one in the depths of his heart—and he would have staked all he possessed to keep it, since in his infatuation he cared for nothing but to keep Tadzio here, and owned to himself not without horror, that he could not exist were the lad to pass from his sight. (53–54)

Passion is identified with evil and disease. The narrator, however, does not pursue the implication that "the bourgeois structure" is to be identified with virtue and health, suggesting perhaps that the structure itself is contaminated by the crime and disease it seeks to suppress. The plague is the city's "evil secret," the truth it wishes to suppress, but perhaps it is a reality that the repressive civic will has itself generated.

Is the "opposition" between form and passion, structure and desire eternal or historically conditioned? By characterizing the structure as bourgeois, Mann suggests a historical condition. But the evidence within the tale itself for a historical interpretation is weak. The Phaedrus myth is an archetype of the drama; that is, it does not depend upon a particular set of social conditions for the career of desire. Nor does Mann elsewhere provide an alternative version of a form or structure that is not repressive.

The career of desire is variously represented. Aschenbach's desire seems to be "satisfied" by the platonic contemplation of Tadzio, an insistence on the pleasures of distance, which promises beyond Tadzio himself "an immensity of richest expectation." His surrender to his passion for Tadzio does not involve a physical consummation. Aschenbach maintains a physical distance from Tadzio, who remains a symbol. Symbolization is itself a function of desire, as Proust makes clear when he speaks of the beloved as the occasion for "an extension of [the] person to all the points in space and time in which the person has occupied and will occupy."[1] Symbolization is the amplification of the object beyond its concrete presence: it is one of the vehicles of desire in the act of writing. Desire itself, not its satisfaction, destroys Aschenbach. The relaxed will, which permits desire to express itself, at times appears to operate under the aegis of Thanatos. Desire takes a more violent form in Aschenbach's dream of a brutal self-degradation. By not confining desire to a single representation, Mann renders the object of desire obscure.

If will is linked to self-control and self-abnegation, it would appear to oppose desire in its self-destructive license; but Mann, I think, discerns an underlying complicity between the two. It is not simply that they are connected through a process of action and reaction (repression and the return of the repressed); they both belong to what Schopenhauer calls the "world of suffering" by virtue of their relentless punishment of the self. Will and desire are two incarnations of the drive toward self-destruction.

Desire demands and resists fulfillment, since no particular fulfillment provides ultimate satisfaction. The dream of desire is illimitable; Aschenbach finds the promise of satisfaction in the limitless ocean.

> His love of the ocean had profound sources: the hard-worked artist's longing for rest, his yearning to seek refuge from the thronging manifold shapes of his fancy in the bosom of the simple and vast; and another yearning, opposed to his art and perhaps for that very reason a lure, for the unorganized, the immeasurable, the eternal—in short, for nothingness. He whose preoccupation is with excellence longs fervently to find rest in perfection; and is not nothingness a form of perfection? (31)

Paradoxically, "the unorganized, the immeasurable . . . nothingness" has become "a form of perfection."

What view does the narrator take of Aschenbach's career? Eric Heller, one of Mann's most acute critics, reads *Death in Venice* as a parody (indeed, a self-parody) of the artistic or aesthetic view of life.

Death in Venice is not only "parody," it is also paradox; a
work of art embodying so radical a critique of art that it amounts
to its moral rejection. . . . It is the speculation of a radical moralist who ironically asserts his moralism in a subject of seemingly
modish morbidity. . . . Gustav Aschenbach, having seemingly
risen beyond suspicion in the disciplined service of art, is brought
down by the revengeful forces of life. . . . What the translation
invariably misses is the ironical elegance and the overtone of
mockery, subtly ridiculing the habitual posturing of the German
language.[2]

Heller does not make entirely clear whether the object of
parody is Aschenbach's severe formalism or his relaxation of the
will. If Aschenbach's formalism is the target, what is the content
of Mann's radical morality? Since the formalism has a moral aspect,
as the narrator himself asserts, then a radical morality must mean
some stark conception of good and evil, virtue and vice, which
does not square with the narrator's sophisticated sensibility. Indeed, the narrator treats the conventional moralizing tendency of
Aschenbach's art severely and sympathizes with his desire for
freedom from its burdens. Heller acknowledges that the matter is
not simple, when he speaks of paradox as well as parody, the
paradox is that the critique of art is embodied by a work of art.
But this is unsatisfactory. Missing from Heller's formulation are
the narrator's persistently ambivalent view of Aschenbach and
Aschenbach's ambivalent view of experience. The presentation of
two kinds of ambivalence (the narrator's and Aschenbach's) helps
us understand how Mann could exempt himself from the judgment
that falls upon Aschenbach, how, in Heller's formulation, Mann
can sustain the paradox of embodying his critique of art within art.

We have already remarked upon Aschenbach's will to form
("And has not form two aspects," the moral and the immoral?)
Elsewhere the ambivalence expresses itself in his experience of
Venice and of Tadzio. Venice is "the incomparable, the fabulous,
the like nothing-else-in the world," it is also a place of narrow
streets, exuding "a hateful sultriness." It is the city of beauty
nonpareil, and a place that is ruled by a predatory commercial
spirit. Tadzio's sickness, which apparently antedates his arrival in
the city, compromises his classic and "chaste beauty." His perfection is tainted with sickliness (his "teeth were imperfect, rather

jagged and bluish, without a healthy glaze, and of that peculiar brittle transparency which the teeth of chlorotic people often show"). The sense of elation that Aschenbach feels in his newfound freedom is checked by the narrator's (and Aschenbach's) sense of its attendant chaos and corruption.

Ambivalence is a word that came into fashion with the advent of psychoanalysis, and it has always been associated with neurotic behavior, that is, with an incapacity for the full and uninhibited expression of erotic feeling. As a point of view in literary discourse, ambivalence suggests not incapacity, but power. It encompasses contradictoriness and conflict. As a mode of contradiction, ambivalence represents an opening to experience, it includes rather than excludes.

Aschenbach acts out his ambivalence, resisting, succumbing, resisting, and finally succumbing. Mann *writes* his ambivalence, never yielding to the temptation while imaginatively experiencing it. Ambivalence in the narrator (in Mann) is a form of control that does not consume itself as it does in Aschenbach, whose control is incapable of accommodating the energies that it tries instead to contain. Ambivalence for Mann becomes a condition for the cathartic exorcism of the demons of desire. It is much more effective than the moralizing art that Heller attributes to Mann, since it allows the energies of will and passion to play themselves out fully and make their claim upon us. The story unfolds with a logic that implies no real alternative to the career of Aschenbach's art and desire. If there is an alternative, it is the writing of *Death in Venice* which assumes the possibility of dividing writing from living. Mann writes his death and thereby survives it.

The problem with ambivalence, Mann's as well as Aschenbach's, is that it assumes a binarism, each term of which offers a dismal prospect, and to which there seems to be no alternative. D. H. Lawrence (aged 24), reviewing *Death in Venice*, characterized Mann "as the last sick sufferer from the complaint of Flaubert," who "regarded life as a disordered corruption against which he can fight with only one weapon, his fine aesthetic sense, his feeling for beauty, for perfection . . . however corrupt the stuff of life may be."[3] The young Lawrence captured the sense of predicament in the tale, to which ambivalence is the logical response. Lawrence's own method, as we shall see in the next chapter, was to imagine alternatives to the oppositions. From the Lawrencean perspective, Mann's ambivalence is confining rather than open.

According to Lawrence, desire cannot be reduced to the status of a term in an opposition that cannot be transcended. Desire, indeed, *becomes* the drive toward the transcendence of opposition. Imagine Aschenbach as an artist of inspiration rather than will, in whom beauty is the satisfaction of desire and not the stimulus of destructive passion, and we have someone approaching the Lawrencean artist.

An alternative that seems unavailable to both Mann and Lawrence is the Christian alternative. In an essay on *Death in Venice,* A. E. Dyson presents a succinct version of the Christian view. Dyson focuses on Aschenbach's homoerotic relationship to Tadzio and addresses the question of why that relationship should destroy Aschenbach. His answer lies in Aschenbach's erotic and obsessive love for Tadzio, which excludes the possibility of another kind of relationship, for instance, friendship. Dyson reads Aschenbach as a Freudian post-Christian man, and he proposes an alternative conception to be found "in Christian life and literature."

> My suggestion, it will be seen, is that friendship—a love rich and pervasive in Christian life and literature—has been the chief casualty of our modern obsession with sex. That our sexual instincts are better understood today is, of course, reassuring, as indeed is our greater tolerance towards deviant sex. But such gains have been won at great cost in confusion and suffering, which Aschenbach's story illustrates especially well. The losses stem from a strange and illogical leap from the understanding that deep love usually arouses sexual feelings, to the dogma that sex is love's root cause and sole end. The next step is the assumption that sexual feelings cannot be vetoed by grace and willpower where they are inappropriate, but that they must be inflamed, rather, until they goad and destroy. This confusion goes back beyond Freud to the early Romantics, and has its distant primitivist precursors in the ancient world. It turns on a view of human relationships which has been a minority report in most periods, but has become overwhelmingly the majority report in the past twenty years. This is the notion that the "self" is the sole source of its own laws and the sole arbiter—its own judge, its own appeal court, its own god. From here, it has followed

that relationships have become a matter of need, not of homage, and increasingly—here modern psychology has certainly been influential—of biological need. The "self" rejecting all external bearings, including good sense and decency, has harvested sexual sufferings on the grandest scale.[4]

Dyson conceives of modern thought and experience as profoundly in error. Aschenbach's predicament and tragedy are based on mistaken assumptions about the nature of human relationships, an attitude he traces back to Freud and back still further to the early Romantics. There are revealing confusions in Dyson's view, which unwittingly help in our understanding of the "necessity" of the tragic career of Aschenbach's desire.

Dyson fails to distinguish between the direct physical expression of homosexual feeling and its sublimated expressions. As we have noted, Aschenbach scrupulously keeps his distance from Tadzio. Nothing in the story authorizes Dyson's assumption that for Aschenbach sex is "love's root cause and end." His love takes place in the imagination. Dyson confounds the relationship between love and sexual feeling on the one hand and between love and friendship on the other. When Dyson speaks of the vetoing of sexual feeling by grace and will power, he could be understood to be speaking of both heterosexual and homosexual love; if so, he would be arguing an ascetic view, which I think irrelevant to a discussion of *Death in Venice*. Certainly, Christianity does not veto sexual feeling: it believes in the moderation of its expression in marriage and its association with love. From a Christian point of view, it is "illicit" and "perverse" love that must be vetoed.

By opposing or contrasting love and friendship, Dyson implies without the candor of explicit statement that friendship should circumscribe the relationship between men. (He could hardly mean to apply the opposition between love and friendship to relationships between men and women.) Dyson's intolerable and repressive view is that homosexuality is sin: that the *love* between men which includes sex "has harvested sufferings on the grandest scale." It is probably fairer to say that the sufferings come from the encounter between desire (in this case of a man for a man) and the socially sanctioned view represented by Dyson.

Dyson's response to Mann's story is illuminating, because it exposes a necessary role that desire performs in life. Homosexual desire should not be confused with the Faustian desire that I describe as a tyranny. It belongs to the host of desires that have a right to satisfaction, the aim of which certainly need not be tyranny over others or self-destruction. Dyson's moralizing against the "self" as the sole source of its own laws is irrelevant to the case at hand.

Aschenbach's failure to consummate his relationship with Tadzio may be read as puritan scruple or as a stubborn commitment to the platonic ladder of love, which seeks to transcend the merely sensual. Either reading makes Aschenbach a moralist to the very core and seems to me to subvert the meaning of his adventure. Aschenbach, I believe, deliberately and scrupulously keeps his distance, because his heroically conceived desire cannot be confined or satisfied by a particular object; it seeks a satisfaction that can only be "achieved" in death. The effect of illimitable desire (a curious paradox) is to repress those particular, limited desires that might satisfy and enhance life. (To be sure, the instance of a consummated love between Aschenbach and the *boy* Tadzio is troublesome, should be troublesome, not because it is homosexual, but because of its inequality and potentiality for exploitation.)

Death in Venice may have invited the confusion between homosexuality and self-destruction by making Tadzio a vehicle of the morbid career of desire. Could it be that Mann's bourgeois prejudice against homosexuality is at work here? If the evil or criminality of passion (in particular, homosexual passion) is defined by "the bourgeois structure" it opposes (Foucault is relevant to this understanding), then we need to hesitate at the very least before making a judgment of Aschenbach's homoerotic feeling for Tadzio, unless we simply wish to identify ourselves with the bourgeois perspective. The culprit, it seems to me, is not Aschenbach's illicit love for Tadzio, but his desire for the illimitable, which as the story makes clear is death itself. Aschenbach's artistic ambition is no longer content with the limited forms of power that require self-repression. He seeks absolute perfection that he ultimately achieves by dying. It is one thing to want to change the boundaries that circumscribe desire (e.g. challenge the norms that condemn homosexuality as a crime against nature), it is another thing to reject the very idea of a boundary, the Faustian ambition (shared by contemporary ideologues) for an illimitable satisfaction.

Dyson speaks of *Death in Venice* as "a triumph of form," though he provides no elucidation. Certainly Aschenbach's example fails: it represses and in the repression exacerbates those energies that it means to control. Like rational logic, artistic form seeks to resolve contradiction, to reconcile opposites, to harmonize elements of conflict. Where the resolution or reconciliation or harmonization goes against "nature," artistic form may represent an exercise of violence: Aschenbach's clenched fist tells us as much. His formal art is an exercise in repression.

If *Death in Venice* represents a triumph of form, we need another conception of form that tolerates and does not conceal contradiction, conflict, the disparateness of experience. In Heller and Dyson, there is a tendency to collapse questions of meaning and form to a single perspective: either moral or aesthetic. But it is the double perspective in perpetual conflict and tension (sympathy and revulsion) that contains the "secret" of the triumph of form in the tale.

In his *Counter-Statement*, Kenneth Burke contrasted "platonic censorship" ("formalistic repressive art" would have served as well) with Aristotle's homeopathic "lightning rod" poetics, which he prefers. "Lightning rods are designed, not to suppress danger, but to draw it into harmless channels."[5] He characterizes the art of Mann and Gide as "a highly fluctuant thing often turning against itself and its own best discoveries. How far it will go, how well it can maintain its characters, I should not venture to calculate."[6] Burke here reproduces in his work Mann's ambivalence toward his own creation. It is the ambivalence of the cathartic artist, who must never confuse the ends of writing and of living. The paradox of the romantic cult of art (as exemplified by Aschenbach's career) is that it wants to liberate desire from the limitations of form. If reason in Kurtz exceeds the bounds of Reason, art in Aschenbach exceeds the bounds of Art. Conrad and Mann write at a moment in European history when the particular set of forms that contain and express life becomes the occasion for a view of the repressiveness of all form, of all limitation. Even in the case where one comes to perceive the necessity of limitation, given the spectacle of the destructive career of unlimited passion, the effect of having opened the floodgates is to render form vulnerable before the deluge. I will now turn to the work of Lawrence, who tried to imagine the emergence of new forms that could contain without diminishing the passional life.

3. ❧ D. H. Lawrence and the Tyranny of Desire

Our most powerful and persistent associations with Lawrence's novels emanate from his portrayal of scenes of sexual passion. But they have often been misread as instances of a liberationist vision. In the cultural imagination, Lawrence is the greatest of our modern professors of desire. This represents a profound misunderstanding of the significance of Lawrence's achievement, in part provoked by Lawrence himself. When, for instance, in opposition to Freud, Lawrence asserts the claim of the passional consciousness (or unconsciousness) against what he views as the repressive character of Freudian psychology, we must be careful how we construe the basic terms of Lawrence's critique. "Character," "personality," "consciousness," "unconsciousness," among other words, Lawrence invested with meanings different from—in some cases opposed to—received understandings of them. A reconsideration of Lawrence's imagination of desire could fruitfully begin with his critique of Freud.

Lawrence's most sustained address to the Freudian conception can be found in two long essays, "Psychoanalysis and the Unconscious" and "Fantasia of the Unconscious." In the first of the essays, Lawrence sets out to distinguish the Freudian unconscious from his own by assigning the Freudian conception to inauthentic neurotic life and his own to the authenticity of creative life. Lawrence does not dismiss the Freudian conception. Rather he places it as a symptom of the condition that psychoanalysis aims to cure.

As Lawrence understands the Freudian unconscious, there are two versions of it that are not exactly consistent with each other. In the first version, the unconscious is a seething, *inchoate* energy of sex and excrement, "Nothing but a slimy serpent of sex, and heaps of excrement, and a myriad repulsive little horrors spawned between sex and excrement";[1] in the second version, the unconscious is the *structure* of the Oedipus complex, that is, the notorious triad of parental-filial relationships in which son, mother, and father love and hate one another. According to Lawrence, the element common to both versions is that they are functions of repression. Rather than an authentic unconscious, they represent projections of a repressive ideal or mental consciousness, which in effect rationalizes its repression of unconscious life by conceiving it as a horror show. "It is nothing pristine and anterior to mentality. It is itself the mind's ulterior motive. That is, the incest-craving is propagated by the mind itself, even though unconsciously."[2] If unconsciousness is a seething cauldron of sex and excrement or a structure of love-hate familial relationships that threaten to become murderous, then repression becomes, in Freud's view, a rational necessity. Freud's thought, in Lawrence's view, becomes a victim of an unnecessary dualism in which the self, poised between a destructive unconscious life and repressive conscious life, is doomed to eternal discontent. Whether one acts out the oedipal drama or represses it, the cost in psychic suffering is great.

Lawrence's own imaginative testimony to the existence of the Oedipus complex is his early autobiographical novel *Sons and Lovers*. There he represents not only his own life, but also the fate of the sons of his generation who had suffered the emasculating effect of parental tyranny, a tyranny that could take the form of weakness (Lawrence's father) as well as strength (his mother). According to Lawrence, the oedipal drama was not the expression of unconscious life, as Lawrence understood the unconscious, but rather of a deliberate, calculated erotic stimulation of the male child by the mother, in turn the consequence of failure of the mother to achieve erotic satisfaction elsewhere—with her husband. At the deepest sensual centers, where authentic unconscious life occurs, Lawrence intuits "a radical sex aversion between parent and child."[3] The consequence of this illicit stimulation of infantile desire is that son, mother, and father hate and love one another in varying forms and degrees of intensity. The son finds he cannot grow up emotionally and sexually and achieve independent manhood, and with a systematic thoroughness possible only to unconscious impulse he displays the same ambivalence in all his other relationships. I use "unconscious impulse" here in the Freudian sense, which Lawrence regarded as an illicit self-justifying invention of mental consciousness. The authentic unconscious—as we encounter it dramatically and poetically in *The Rainbow* and *Women in Love*—is the dark, fecund source of creativity, an energy constitutive of new forms, new selves. The provenance of the Lawrencean unconscious is the muse of romantic poetry and religious inspiration.

Lawrence's essays on psychoanalysis can be read as a double narrative of psychological development, one proceeding from the "authentic" creative unconscious, the other from the neurotic arrested unconscious. According to Lawrence, Freud's psychology of the unconscious is an accurate description of *neurotic* life and is qualitatively different from authentic unconscious life. Freud would not have tolerated *such* a dualism if only because he held (and it was an essential tenet of his science) that normality and neurosis exist in a continuum.

Lawrence characterizes the destruction of the individual as the consequence of the hypertrophy of the love mode. The dynamic connection between parent and child, originating from what Lawrence calls the "lower planes of consciousness," is perpetually denied by the upper sympathetic planes. "Where there is too much sympathy, then the great voluntary [lower] centers of the spine are weak, the child tends to be delicate."[4] Normal development originates from the lower centers (the solar plexus, for example) and moves upwards. The spontaneous passional centers determine the activities of will and mind in a healthy person. In contrast, neurotic development originates from the mind and moves downward in order to achieve repressive control of the lower centers. "That which sublimates from the dynamic consciousness into mental consciousness has alone any value. . . . Every extraneous idea which has no root in the dynamic consciousness is as dangerous as a nail driven into a tree."[5]

It would seem to follow from his stress on the *lower* centers that Lawrence would be an advocate of spontaneity and passion at the expense of the reason and the will—that his doctrine would be in opposition to exercises of reason and will. But such a reading radically simplifies and distorts Lawrence's position. To be sure, Lawrence affirms spontaneity and darkness. But they are put in a surprising association with values that are normally connected with reason and the will, the upper centers of consciousness. The lower centers are the sources of resistance, the upper centers of love and sympathy. And the resistant mode is that of self-definition and self-responsibility, whereas the love mode is that of mingling and the loss of identity.

The stress on the resistant mode and the mistrust of sympathy and love devalues the sexual motive. Lawrence does not deny the sexual motive, but neither does he give it primacy in the unconscious. It is not the be-all and end-all, Lawrence asserts with a polemical vigor which suggests that such a view is a threatening reality. "The essentially religious or creative motive is the first motive for all human activity. The sexual motive comes second." The religious or creative motive provides energy for the making of civilization: "the desire of the human male to build a world . . . to build up out of his own self and his own belief and his own effort something wonderful."[6] The effect of this inversion of the psychoanalytic hierarchy of motive is to reconceive the problem of the relation of the passions to civilized life, as we find it formulated in Freud and Mann. Civilization, in Lawrence's view, is not the product of repression, but is rather the expression of the creative unconscious. The experience of repression is the consequence of a betrayal of authentic unconscious life by an inauthentic unconscious that is no more than a projection of the interests of what Lawrence calls "mental consciousness." Lawrence is one of the first, if not the first critic of the hypothesis of repression; that is, he denies the view that repression is intrinsic to the nature and history of civilized life. He does not deny the fact of repression, but only its privileged status in Freudian thought as a category of understanding of civilization.

But what are we to make of the devaluation of the sexual motive in Lawrence's work? It is omnipresent in his fiction and his discursive writing and it makes one wonder how Lawrence came to be regarded as a champion of sexual freedom. Indeed, perhaps no writer surpasses Lawrence in the keenness of his imaginative awareness of the *threat* of the passional life. Even in the scenes of passion, when it is tempting to read a celebration of the event, the sense of threat is so powerful that it subverts a simple affirmative reading.

Consider an early scene in *The Rainbow*, in which Tom Brangwen and Lydia make love for the first time:

> A daze had come over his mind, he had another center of consciousness. In his breast, or in his bowels, somewhere in his body, there had started another activity. It was as if a strong light were burning there, and he was blind within it, unable to know anything, except that this transfiguration burned between him and her, connecting them, like a secret power.
>
> Since she had come to the house he went about in a daze, scarcely seeing even the things he handled, drifting, quiescent, in a state of metamorphosis. He submitted to that which was happening to him, letting go his will, suffering the loss of himself, dormant always on the brink of ecstasy, like a creature evolving to a new birth.*

The setting is a dark, virtually invisible space in which the lovers are swept by a passion felt in the breasts and the bowels. The language describing the scene is the language of suffering. It is a kind of religious passion, a dissolution of an old self and the birth of a new. The stages are the familiar ones of suffering, sleep, and reawakening or rebirth. These are demanding conditions, an extraordinary burden for the sexual act. One might read the scene as a religious event, a scene of fulfillment. And certainly in later

---

* D. H. Lawrence, *The Rainbow* (1915) (New York: Viking, 1961), p. 33. Subsequent references in the text are given with the abbreviation *R* and the page number.

scenes, their coming together occurs in a transcendent realm, a divine space, inaccessible to ordinary lovers.

> They had passed through the doorway into the further space, where movement was so big, that it contained bonds and constraints and labours, and still was complete liberty. She was the doorway to him, he to her. At last they had thrown open the doors, each to the other, and had stood in the doorways facing each other, whilst the light flooded out from behind on to each of their faces, it was the transfiguration, glorification, the admission. (*R*, 91)

But the fulfillment already possesses the knowledge of its impossible burden, its self-destructiveness. The novel opens with a contrast between the Brangwen men and women which realizes the destructiveness of a life devoted to sensual passion.

> [The Brangwen women] faced outwards to where men moved dominant and creative, having turned their back on the pulsing heat of creation, and with this behind them, were set out to discover what was beyond, to enlarge their own scope and range and freedom; whereas the Brangwen men faced inwards to the teeming life of creation, which poured unresolved into their veins. (*R*, 3)

At the end of chapter 3, "The Childhood of Anna Lensky," Tom Brangwen is "the broken arch" (*R*, 92), a man whose dependence on his lover is complete, who, in the grandiloquent religious language of the novel, looks inward to the teeming life of creation and is consumed by it. Later in the novel (in "The March and the Flood"), Tom drowns in a flood, in language that recalls his consuming relationship to Lydia: "He went to meet the running flood, sinking deeper and deeper. His soul was full of great astonishment. He had to go and look where it came from . . ." (*R*, 243). Passion can destroy and consume.

If we read *The Rainbow* as Lawrence's version of *Paradise Lost*, then we can see the failed or lost innocence of the first generation as a failure according to a life of passion.[7] Indeed, each successive generation, Tom and Lydia, Will and Anna Brangwen, Ursula and Anton Skrebensky shows the self-destructive course of passion, the only alternative to which is self-responsibility, autonomous being, a kind of paradise regained.

Religious rapture has often expressed itself through erotic language, subverting the ascetic strain in puritanical religion. In Donne and Herbert, for example, the erotic could be a via media to the divine as well as a diversion from it. In the failure of organized religion to provide fulfillment, eros becomes the "site" of the spiritual life, but its fulfillment more often than not turns out to be a terrifying experience. Lawrence half-discovered (I don't think he became fully cognizant of all that he imagined) that neither the sexual encounter nor the lover could bear the full weight of religious rapture. The agony, the shattering impact on the self (so far from the pleasures of sex) becomes as much a thing to be dreaded as desired.

The task of achieving autonomy (what Birkin in *Women in Love* will call "paradisal entry into pure, single being")* falls to a third-generation Brangwen: Ursula. Self-responsibility for Ursula (and for the self-responsible heroes and heroines in the later work) is the mode of resistance that Lawrence describes in the essays on psychoanalysis. In effect Lawrence postulates two orders of desire, the desire for mingling, for love, for identity with the other and the desire to stand alone, to be oneself, Lawrence preferring the desire for autonomy. Ursula remains a Brangwen: her "salvation" at the end, the hope evidenced by the rainbow, depends upon her recovery of the Brangwen energy that for a time seems to have deserted her in the modern industrialized world. But "salvation" depends upon a paradoxical play of the energy against itself.

We see this most graphically in a scene toward the end of *The Rainbow* in which Ursula imagines horses stampeding her soul. The episode follows an act of potential self-betrayal: Ursula is prepared to give herself to Anton Skrebensky, a lover whom she had previously rejected, from a fearful anxiety that she had been arrogantly wicked in wanting to create her own self. "What did the self, the form of life matter. Only the living from day to day mattered . . . no beyond, no further trouble, no further complications" (*R*, 483). The horses appear as a terrifying reminder of her deepest desire to create her own self. They thunder upon her, frighten her, triumph. She runs from them in terror, "in a flame of

* D. H. Lawrence, *The Rainbow* (1915) (New York: Viking, 1961), p. 33. Subsequent references in the text are given with the abbreviation *R* and the page number.

agony" climbs a knotted oak, falls from the branch and continues to run. "Her will alone carried her" (R, 489). The stampede causes an illness which brings her to the verge of death ("she lay as if unconscious upon the bed of the stream") and from which she emerges strengthened, resolute, confident in her separateness. The horses incarnate a violent purification in which the self, Ursula's self, is free to imagine a civilization of "new, clean, naked bodies [which] would issue to a new germination, to a new growth . . ." (R, 495).

The horses represent the Brangwen energy in its physical beauty and passion. The scene (aggression, resistance, possession) has a sexual resonance, but it also serves to renounce sexuality in the forms it has taken in Ursula's life—in particular with Skrebensky and Ursula's teacher Winifred Inger. Ursula's passionate desire is to be herself against all the solicitations of those desires that would diminish and disintegrate her.

The desire for autonomy, for a self-possessed solitude can be understood as a defense against the importunities of desire. To be autonomous is to constitute one's own world, create one's desires, and control their satisfaction. In order to achieve this autonomy, the self must assert its superiority and indifference to the world. In *The Rainbow,* Ursula makes precisely this assertion when she denies reality to the town:

> It does not exist really. It rests upon the unlimited darkness, like
> a gleam of colored oil on dark water, but what is it—nothing,
> just nothing. (R, 477–78)

The contest between self and world, however, is unequal, a mismatch in which the individual is doomed to defeat, if he chooses to remain within the social arena. Lawrence knew this and tried to insulate the self from society in his theory of the self as "intrinsically other." That is, he imagines the self as an intransitive structure of being, behaving according to its own spiritual necessity without reference to the social ideal.

Such autonomy, however, is an illusion and Lawrence betrays his knowledge of this by invoking divine or demonic presences. Lawrence's use of a religious language to express personal states of consciousness is not merely metaphorical. It reflects a traditional belief that the autonomous self is an insufficiency. Unlike Dostoevsky, however, who could still find in the Russian Orthodox Church spiritual sustenance, Lawrence had to reimagine or reinvent figures of divinity grounded in the religious or mythical life of the pre-Christian era. If the god-talk in his work is unconvincing, it is not because Lawrence misunderstood the modern need, but because the myths and religions that sustain individuals and societies cannot be fabricated by acts of individual imagination.

The struggle to be oneself will continue in *Women in Love*, where it receives the most complex and puzzling expressions. The world according to Birkin at the beginning of *Women in Love* is a bleaker version of the world according to Ursula at the beginning of *The Rainbow*. It is at the moment of apocalypse, and what is at stake is the survival and integrity of the self. In *The Rainbow*, Ursula "knew that the sordid people who crept hard-scaled and separate on the face of the world's corruption were living still" (*R*, 495). In *Women in Love*, the world is corrupt and hollow: "not many people are anything at all. . . . It would be better if they were wiped out." Unlike Ursula's apocalyptic vision at the conclusion of *The Rainbow*, Birkin's misanthropic and genocidal language is not immediately qualified by the language of hope:

> "People don't really matter," he said, rather unwilling to continue.
> The mother [Mrs. Crich] looked up at him with sudden, dark interrogation, as if doubting his sincerity.
> "How do you mean, *matter?*" she asked sharply.
> "Not many people are anything at all," he answered, forced to go deeper than he wanted to. "They jingle and giggle. It would be much better if they were just wiped out. Essentially, they don't exist, they aren't there."
> She watched him steadily while he spoke.
> "But we don't imagine them," she said sharply.
> "There's nothing to imagine, that's why they don't exist."
> "Well," she said, "I would hardly go as far as that. There they are, whether they exist or no. It doesn't rest with me to decide on their existence. I only know that I can't be expected to take *account* of them all. You can't expect me to know them, just because they happen to be there. As far as *I* go they might as well not be there." (*WL*, 18–19)

Birkin hates what he views as the will-dominated, mechanical world and wants to recover *spontaneous* being, not its false facsimiles. If he rejects people in general, he repudiates the female, in particular the will-dominated female. His lover Hermione, who thinks and speaks in the idiom of spontaneity, is a creature of willful violence. Birkin, provocateur of character, provokes Hermione to an act of violence (in a mindless rage she strikes him with a ball of lapis lazuli), which effectively frees Birkin not only of Hermione, but of the demand for love that seems to him to be a generic female demand. Love, will, disintegration constitute a strange combination in Lawrencean logic.

Birkin's repudiation of the female, however, is only partial. Birkin will form a powerful, though turbulent, connection with Ursula, but the main drama of their relationship will be Birkin's effort to establish its conditions. He wants a connection with her in which his selfhood is inviolable. He resists what he experiences as her desire to possess him, to mingle with him in love. In the Breadalby episode, Birkin asserts the doctrine of "disquality"—a word that Birkin invents to represent a desired condition of radical *independence* and *incomparability* of the individual, a condition to be distinguished in political and social terms from aristocratic notions of domination and subordination and democratic notions of equality.

> "But I, myself, who am myself, what have I to do with equality with any other man or woman? In the spirit, I am as separate as one star is from another, as different in quality and quantity. Establish a state on *that*. One man isn't any better than another, not because they are equal, but because they are intrinsically *other*, that there is no term of comparison. The minute you begin to compare, one man is seen to be far better than another, all the inequality you can imagine is there by nature. I want every man to have his share in the world's goods, so that I am rid of his importunity, so that I can tell him: 'Now you've got what you want—you've got your fair share of the world's gear. Now, you one-mouthed fool, mind yourself and don't obstruct me.' " (*WL*, 96–97)

The sexual correlative of disquality is figured by Birkin in "the star equilibrium" in which the independence of the sexual self is preserved even in the act of love.

"What I want is a strange conjunction with you—" he said quietly; "—not meeting and mingling;—you are quite right:—but an equilbrium, a pure balance of two single beings:—as the stars balance each other." (*WL,* 139)

That is, Birkin tries to redefine the act of love so as to exclude its disintegrative tendency. The sexual act ceases to be an act of mingling, of surrender and becomes instead an act of separation. The male and female make love in the mode of resistance.

In the first volume of *The History of Sexuality,* Michel Foucault attacks the tyranny of sexual desire (what he calls "the deployment of sexuality") and calls to his support the following passage from Lawrence. "There has been so much action in the past, especially sexual action, a wearying repetition over and over, without a corresponding thought, a corresponding realization. Now our business is to realize sex. Today the full conscious realization of sex is even more important than the act itself."[8] The "conscious realization" for both Foucault and Lawrence is that sexuality has become "the hidden aspect and generative principle of meaning,"[9] the tyrannical essence of man and woman, depriving them of the imagination of other life possibilities. Lawrence before Foucault means to preserve the life of the body against the efforts of sexuality to usurp and define it.

At the conclusion of *Fantasia of the Unconscious,* in the spirit of Birkin's own diatribes, Lawrence explicitly attacks what he believes to be the sexual metaphysic of psychoanalytic theory, which he suggests is a legacy of the romantic cult of passion.

> The sex goal needs, absolutely needs, this further departure. And if there be no further departure, no great way of belief on ahead: and if sex is the starting point and the goal as well: the sex becomes like the bottomless pit, insatiable. It demands at last the departure into death, the only available beyond. Like Carmen, or like Anna Karenina. When sex is the starting point and the returning point both, the only issue is death. Which is plain as pike-staff in *Carmen* or *Anna Karenina* and is the theme of all modern tragedy.[10]

Such a strong, some might say hysterical, attack, on the tyranny of sexuality could not be made if the person or character making the attack did not feel so threatened or susceptible. And

Women in Love provides telling, though perplexing, evidence of Lawrence's protagonist's (and his own) susceptibility. The episodes "Moony" and "Gladiatorial" form a particularly vivid sequence.

In "Moony" Birkin returns from his self-imposed exile in Europe to Willey Pond, where he comes upon the reflection of the moon on the water. For Birkin, the moon is "Cybele," "Syria Dea," goddess of the feminine, tyrannical mother and lover. In a fit of violence, Birkin throws stones at the moon's reflection which then becomes "a white body of fire writhing and striving," but "not even now broken open, not yet violated" (*WL*, 239). The symbolic event makes clear that the authority of the feminine will reconstitute and reassert itself, that the moon remains "inviolable." The episode is given to us from Ursula's perspective who, unbeknownst to Birkin, is present at the scene, and not only present as a witness, but also as a victim, shattered by what she witnesses.

> Ursula was dazed, her mind was all gone. She felt she had fallen to the ground and was spilled out, like water on the earth. Motionless and spent she remained in the gloom. Though even now she was aware, unseeing, that in the darkness was a little tumult of ebbing flakes of light, a cluster dancing secretly in a round, twining and coming steadily together. (*WL*, 240)

But like the "distorted, frayed" moon that regains its wholeness and composure, Ursula regains hers and confronts Birkin. He is bemused by her challenge about his hatred of the moon: "Why should you hate the moon? It hasn't done you any harm, has it?" (*WL*, 241). "Was it hate?" he wonders aloud, suggesting that he may not be in full possession of his feelings, that he does not know what he is doing. Perhaps Birkin discharges anger in order to free himself to love Ursula, for he reluctantly admits that he loves her.

Or perhaps it is with an act of persistent "feminine" resentment that Ursula refuses to accept the conditions that he has laid down for a relationship, conditions expressed in the figure of "the star equilibrium." In Birkin's view, Ursula refuses to drop her assertive will and let go (*WL*, 179). Ursula sees it the other way around: it is Birkin who can't let go, who can't trust himself implicitly. And Birkin, consistent with the mood of uncertainty that has overtaken him, admits the possibility that he may be wrong.

> The next day, however, he felt wistful and yearning. He thought he had been wrong, perhaps. Perhaps he had been wrong to go to her with an idea of what he wanted. Was it really only an idea, or was it the interpretation of a profound yearning? If the latter, how was it he was always talking about sensual fulfilment? The two did not agree very well. (*WL*, 245)

At the very least, the Moony episode suggests that we should not trust implicitly Birkin's version of the events.

Birkin's doctrine of spontaneity contradicts his laying down the conditions of relationship, even a relationship which he sees as necessary to spontaneity itself. Lawrence's protagonists from Birkin on are given a bully pulpit to expound their views and to coerce others to change their lives. Lawrence and his heroes affirm the overriding importance of spontaneity, which they then lay as a compulsion on others. Be yourself, but let me tell you what I know to be the true conditions of selfhood.

The narrative passes to a memory of a West African fetish that Birkin had once seen. In the Crème de Menthe episode, Birkin had been shown a female figurine, which is now made to bear an enormous symbolic weight.

> She knew what he himself did not know. She had thousands of years of purely sensual, purely unspiritual knowledge behind her. It must have been thousands of years since her race had died, mystically: that is, since the relation between the senses and the outspoken mind had broken, leaving the experience all in one sort, mystically sensual. Thousands of years ago, that which was imminent in himself must have taken place in these Africans: the goodness, the holiness, the desire for creation and productive happiness must have lapsed, leaving the single impulse for knowledge in one sort, mindless progressive knowledge through the senses, knowledge arrested and ending in the senses, mystic knowledge in disintegration and dissolution, knowledge such as the beetles have, which live purely within the world of corruption and cold dissolution. This was why her face looked like a beetle's: this was why the Egyptians worshipped the ball-rolling scarab: because of the principle of knowledge in dissolution and corruption. (*WL*, 245–46)

71

In the Moony episode, the African fetish abruptly evokes thoughts of Gerald's destructive "ice-consciousness" and a speculation about an alternative way of being, what he calls: "free proud singleness" (*WL*, 247). Leaving aside the question of the aesthetic justification for these abrupt shifts of focus, there is the more interesting question of the psycho-logic of these narrative shifts. What is the relevance of these shifts to his relationship with Ursula?

Birkin fears that a passionate love for Ursula will lead to his reduction and disintegration into pure sensuality that he has imagined in the presence of the African figure. This view is confirmed by the passage in which he speaks of "destructive creation" and "universal dissolution."

> When the stream of synthetic creation lapses, we find ourselves part of the inverse process, the blood of destructive creation. Aphrodite is born in the first spasm of universal dissolution —then the snakes and swans and lotus—marsh-flowers—and Gudrun and Gerald—born in the process of destructive creation. (*WL*, 164)

The sense of threat seems exaggerated, the vision hallucinatory and hysterical. Indeed, it has been argued that Birkin's anger masks a fear, an anxiety about his sexual identity. Birkin's proposal to Ursula at the end of "Moony" sets conditions that violate Ursula's self-respect. One might speculate that Birkin, perhaps only half-aware, wants her to refuse his offer. Rejected by Ursula, he leaves Beldover and goes directly to Gerald in a "whirl of fury" (*WL*, 258).

In "Gladiatorial" Gerald and Birkin will strip naked and engage in a wrestling match that has an erotic intensity unmatched in the novel.

> So the two men entwined and wrestled with each other, working nearer and nearer. Both were white and clear, but Gerald flushed smart red where he was touched, and Birkin remained white and tense. He seemed to penetrate into Gerald's more solid, more diffuse bulk, to interfuse his body through the body of the other, as if to bring it subtly into subjection, always seizing with some rapid necromantic foreknowledge every motion of the other flesh, converting and counteracting it, playing

upon the limbs and trunk of Gerald like some hard wind. It was as if Birkin's whole physical intelligence interpenetrated into Gerald's body, as if his fine, sublimated energy entered into the flesh of the fuller man, like some potency, casting a fine net, a prison, through the muscles into the very depths of Gerald's physical being. (*WL*, 262)

The wrestling, represented as a kind of male bonding (a blood brotherhood), is so charged with homosexual suggestion that it would be sophistical and misleading to deny it, as some critics have done. But the question remains: what is the significance of Birkin's homoeroticism? The psychoanalytic view, for instance, that the "star equilibrium" is a rationalization serving homosexual desire and that Birkin's ideas about the inviolateness of the male self conceal or express a deep and abiding mistrust of women may be part of the truth. But the normative Freudian idiom of such a judgment diverts us from the risk that Lawrence has taken in presenting the scene.

Birkin and Gerald do *not* enter into an explicitly sexual relationship. Birkin returns to Ursula to achieve a not entirely convincing fulfillment, rather a strange god-like or king-like satisfaction of desire.

> . . . she had a full mystic knowledge of his suave loins of darkness, dark-clad and suave, and in this knowledge there was some of the inevitability and the beauty of fate, fate which one asks for, which one accepts in full.
>
> He sat still like an Egyptian Pharaoh, driving the car. He felt as if he were seated in immemorial potency, like the great carven statues of real Egypt, as real and as fulfilled with subtle strength, as these are, with a vague inscrutable smile on the lips. He knew what it was to have the strange and magical current of force in his back and loins, and down his legs, force so perfect that it stayed him immobile, and left his face subtly, mindlessly smiling. He knew what it was to be awake and potent in that other basic mind, the deepest physical mind. And from this source he had a pure and magic control, magical, mystical, a force in darkness, like electricity. (*WL*, 310)

This deeply awful rhetoric betrays the stridency, the substitution of the wish for the reality. As a fantasy of power, not sexual pleasure, it anticipates the power fantasies and political obsessions

73

of the later novels, *Kangaroo* and *The Plumed Serpent*. Desire in Birkin, as in Lawrence, becomes an ungratified will to power.

To explain the presence of sexuality, whatever form it takes in Lawrence's work, we have to address the transgressive character of his artistic imagination. Indeed, what is interesting about Birkin's relationship with Gerald is precisely its transgressive character. Lawrence has penetrated the defenses and seized or has been seized by the explosive character of a socially, morally uncensored sexuality. The result is a report from the front. And the effect is ambivalence. In penetrating the defenses, in transgressing boundaries, Lawrence experiences the necessity for resistance. He has learned at firsthand the tyranny of desire. Lawrence, the political and social anarchist, does not extend his anarchism to the regime of the self. On the contrary, Lawrence wishes to reconstitute and preserve it.

Transgression is the artist's privilege. The artist and his/her art appear sporadically in *Women in Love,* achieving its most interesting expression in the appearance of Loerke, a futurist painter, modeled on Lawrence's acquaintance Max Gertler. He is a formalist and abstractionist, who believes in the absolute separation of art and life. In the somewhat fatuous quarrel between Loerke and Ursula about the status of a horse in a work of art, Loerke insists that the horse is *not* a horse: it is not a living organism but a form, a familiar enough view of early modernism. If there is an inspiration in "life" for Loerke's art, it is the machine. Loerke is a follower of the futurist Marinetti, for whom the machine was a model against the romantic aesthetics based on organic form.

Ursula, apparently speaking for Lawrence, insists that art gives us the truth of real life. It is mere assertion on her part, and she sounds naive in contrast to Loerke's sophistication. Between naivete and sophistication, we are intended to prefer Ursula's virtuous naivete to Loerke's corrupt sophistication. He is granted an intellectual, even intuitive penetration, a power to know the soul of another, but knowledge here is corrosive and devouring, frightening and fascinating. "[Gudrun] knew what he was unconscious of, his tremendous power of understanding, of apprehending her living motion. He did not know his own power. He did not know how, with his full, submerged, watchful eyes, he could look into her and see her, what she was, see her secrets. He would only want her to be herself—he knew her verily, with a subconscious, sinister knowledge, devoid of illusions and hopes" (*WL*, 417). Like the machine-dominated Gerald Crich, Loerke is a creature of negative will who, however, possesses an artistic subtlety that enables him to penetrate the inner recesses of Gudrun's being, a feat Gerald is incapable of. "There was only the inner, individual darkness, sensation within the ego, the obscene religious mystery of ultimate reduction, the mystic frictional activities of diabolic reducing down, disintegrating the vital organic body of life" (*WL*, 443).

Ursula's hatred of Loerke, which seems to have the endorsement of the narrator, however, should not blind us to the Loerke element in Lawrence's artistic intelligence. Loerke is the transgressor, the deepest explorer of disintegrative sexual experience in the novel. In *Women in Love*, the sexual imagination *in extremis* is associated with the machine, not with organic life. Sex as an all-absorbing activity is another form of self-alienation. Witness the terrible loneliness of Gerald, king of the mines, sexual conquerer, who is ultimately vanquished.

The imagination of *Women in Love* is devoted to the resistance to all the destructive "hegemonic" impulses in life; the ascendancy of any mode of existence, of any particular energy or faculty. Lawrence understood as well as anyone the tyranny of sexual desire, which he had already found in full display in the nineteenth century heroines of passion: Emma Bovary, Anna Karenina, Iseult, and Carmen, each consumed with and destroyed by passion.

Lawrence tries to imagine an escape from the world of self-destructive passion: this is the utopian aim of his art. The mimetic view says that art imitates already enacted life, the formalist view that art has nothing to do with life. The Lawrencean view asserts that art can imagine new forms of life. Consider the following exchange between Ursula and Gudrun:

> "I think," she said at length, involuntarily, "that Rupert is right—one wants a new space to be in, and one falls away from the old."
> Gudrun watched her sister with impassive face and steady eyes.
> "One wants a new space to be in, I quite agree," she said.

"But *I* think that a new world is a development from this world, and that to isolate oneself with one other person, isn't to find a new world at all, but only to secure oneself in one's illusions."

Ursula looked out of the window. In her soul she began to wrestle, and she was frightened. She was always frightened of words, because she knew that mere word-force could always make her believe what she did not believe.

"Perhaps," she said, full of mistrust, of herself and everybody. "But," she added, "I do think that one can't have anything new whilst one cares for the old—do you know what I mean?—even fighting the old is belonging to it. I know, one is tempted to stop with the world, just to fight it. But then it isn't worth it."

Gudrun considered herself.

"Yes," she said. "In a way, one is of the world if one lives in it. But isn't it really an illusion to think you can get out of it? After all, a cottage in the Abruzzi, or wherever it may be, isn't a new world. No, the only thing to do with the world is to see it through." (*WL*, 428–29)

Ursula wants a new space. Gudrun responds sensibly and realistically when she says the old forms of life would persist in the new space. Who is right? Ursula does not have an answer, but our sympathies are with her. Words may be persuasive in repressing energies and blocking possibility and they may be frightening in their persuasiveness.

But Lawrence and his surrogates Birkin and Ursula do not want to surrender language to the repressors. The new space they want is represented by the language that we have come to know in *The Rainbow:* the inhuman, the impersonal, that which transcends the social and the personal and which may be evoked by a religious and mystical vocabulary. Should we trust *this* language? Isn't it engaged in an impossible task of trying to represent the unrepresentable? Moreover, Lawrence refuses to subscribe to the division between writing and living, a division that licenses imaginative experiments in the impossible. He wants to write out the creative unconscious and realize its forms of life.

What is it that empowers Birkin, Ursula and, for that matter, Lawrence to imagine and realize this new space? Differences in the characterizations of Gerald and Birkin are revealing. Gerald is a social creation; we see him as formed by his family and his struggle with it; we see him the master but ultimately the victim of the mines. Birkin, on the other hand, seems not to be socially constructed, not formed by the conventional moral scheme. He seems to be without a family. His social group may perhaps be defined by the Bohemians, the dilettantish artists and hangers on who appear in "Crème de Menthe" (Halliday et al.), but Birkin doesn't really belong. There is a spiritual dimension that suggests no social space in the actual world. He is more like a messianic figure come to save individuals and redeem relationships.

Perhaps a consideration of the historical setting in which Lawrence writes the novel would be relevant here. *Women in Love* was published in 1920, just after World War I, an event that registers in Birkin's apocalyptic mood at the beginning of the novel. It is the end of an era, of a society. The social and domestic pieties seem to have lost their authority. There is a sense of social disintegration that frees a creative character like Birkin to imagine new possibilities, but in this case the imagination of possibilities is confined to the cultivation of individuality, personal relationships, or relationships vis-à-vis a mystically charged natural world.

Birkin expresses contempt for a world composed of couples (he characterizes the couple as an *egoisme à deux*) (*WL*, 344), but the Lawrencean world is essentially one of couples or of isolated figures mystically converted to the natural world. Indeed, Ursula feels "authorized" in her quest for the new space by her experience of love in the old one. So she can feel scorn for Gudrun's implicit claim for love ("Well, I've got no further than love, yet") with the thought: "Because you never *have* loved, you can't get beyond it" (*WL*, 430). Much as Lawrence wanted to see the emergence of a new society, he could not imagine one.

The illusory character of the art-life continuum, as Lawrence-Ursula understands it, becomes clear when we consider Lawrence's adversarial role as an artist. In their combat with modern life, Lawrence and his protagonists perform deliberate acts of self-alienation from family, community, society, "real life." Lawrence was as much the alienated artist as any formalist modernist. In this fashion, he conceived his task as the reconception of the whole world in his consciousness. When Ursula (in *The Rainbow*) says that reality is in me and the external world, the rest of the world is *nothing*, when Birkin condemns the world to destruction, because mankind is contemptible, they are in effect enacting a version of the "aesthetic" repudiation of the world. The tyranny Lawrence did not escape, of which he was not fully conscious, was the modern desire for an absolute self, radically other, free of all constraints, beyond comparison, alone in a mythical cosmos.

> We ought to dance with rapture that we should be alive and in the flesh, and part of the living incarnate cosmos. I am part of the sun as my eye is part of me. That I am part of the earth my feet know perfectly, and my blood is part of the sea. My soul knows that I am part of the human race, my soul is an organic part of the great human soul, as my spirit is part of my nation. In my own very self, I am part of my family. There is nothing of me that is alone and absolute except my mind, and we shall find that the mind has no existence by itself, it is only the glitter of the sun on the surface of the waters.[11]

Lawrence opposes an ecstatic, onanistic aloneness (don't be deceived by his insistence that he is not alone) in which the self absorbs and is enhanced by the cosmos to the romantic cult of passion, the dissolution of the identities of lovers into a death-like unity. Lawrence discovers the terror at the heart of sexual passion. By isolating his characters, Lawrence means to make them free from all the codes and forms that make for character (Lawrence would disparagingly call it "personality") the effect of which, if successful, permits a socially undetermined desire to fill up the entire space of the psyche. But *his* passion for autonomy carries with it its own risks of the terrors of isolation. Lawrence remains a tragic figure, who experienced and saw more deeply than any of his English contemporaries the destructive energies of modern life, but whose alternative imagination of an isolate "self-responsibility" left him exposed to the very energies he fought to master.

Lawrence's commitment to the creative unconscious is an attempt to overcome the tragic dualism that informs the work of Freud and Mann. I don't think that Lawrence believed that he fully succeeded in this attempt, but his faith in the creative unconscious as utopian possiblity persisted. Lawrence's imagination of desire, however, has a Faustian aspect that produces a sense of unresolvable tension and conflict. What is moving in Lawrence's work is the conflict between his realism about insatiable desire and his utopian belief in its fulfillment.

4. What Dowell Knew: A Reading of Ford's *The Good Soldier*

Conrad, Mann, and Lawrence present heroic figures of desire. Kurtz, Aschenbach, and Birkin are men with callings. They are driven by an ambition to perform exemplary deeds. Their lives are what Karl Jaspers called "representative destinies." Their fates constitute the fate of our culture. With Ford Madox Ford, we enter the more familiar world of modern pathos. The world of *The Good Soldier* announces its failure at the outset. "This is the saddest story I have ever heard."* It is as if the characters of the novel have known from the very beginning of their conscious lives that desire is aimless, futile, sheer suffering. Like his contemporaries, Ford imagines desire, unlimited and unconstrained by codes and forms of social life.

At the beginning of *The Good Soldier*, the narrator John Dow-

---

* Ford Madox Ford, *The Good Soldier* (1927) (New York: Vintage, 1983), p. 3. All subsequent references are in the text.

ell establishes the equivocal, if not contradictory, mode of his narration. He knew the Ashburnhams "with an extreme intimacy" and yet he "knew nothing at all about them." The narration does not mark a progress from ignorance to knowledge. "When I sit down to puzzle out what I know of this sad affair I knew nothing whatever." This is a somewhat confusing shift in tense from "know" to "knew," for there is no real difference between what he knew about the Ashburnhams nine seasons earlier—when he and his wife first met them—and what he knows now. The saddest truth in this the saddest story is that he "know[s] nothing—nothing in the world—of the hearts of men" (7). Yet the story he tells is about "hearts" passionate but diseased, too frail to survive the shocks of their own passions.

One is tempted to ascribe Dowell's ignorance to his utter failure as a sexual being. What could this "eunuch" be expected to know of characters like Edward, Leonora, and his own wife Florence, since unlike them he had never been touched by passion? I think Ford means us to take the opposite view: Dowell's freedom from passion gives him a more or less disinterested eye, a capacity to contemplate the spectacle of the passions of others without being unduly unsettled by them. He is the Negatively Capable narrator, whose personality is the vehicle for others to manifest their own personalities. Dowell is not the venal unreliable narrator, whose moral and sexual deficiencies are the subject of the novel.[1] Rather, he is a device who makes possible the exploration of the passionate lives of others. Since Dowell is a participant in the drama, one of the four that "danced the minuet" and a cuckold, the victim of an awful deception, Ford must assure his objectivity by neutralizing his passions. "You ask how it feels to be a deceived husband. Just heavens, I do not know. It feels just nothing" (70). Whatever we may think of a man, incapable of feeling the humiliation of having been cuckolded, is irrelevant to the narrative necessity of guaranteeing Dowell's cold eye. Dowell shows how secure he is from the deformations of passion when he characterizes his apparently genuine attachment to Nancy in an astonishing simile: "I want to marry [Nancy] as some people go to Carcasonne" (121).

I don't mean to deprive Dowell of his status as a character by speaking of him as a device. His lack of sexual passion or susceptibility to sexual humiliation may indeed be read as *accidia*, "the dull hysteria of sloth . . . the sluggish insanity of defective love," as Mark Schorer characterizes it.[2] And for all his apparent indifference to the humiliation that he has suffered at the hands of his wife, he is on more than one occasion venomously unforgiving of her. When she dies, he speaks of her as having had no more reality than a piece of paper. Dowell's feelings and responses are ambivalent and inconsistent. On more than one occasion, Dowell speaks of himself as a "dual personality, the one I being entirely unconscious of the other" and he observes himself talking "in an odd way, as people do who are recovering from an anaesthetic" (103). But he is nevertheless a device in that his character permits Ford to achieve the effect of cold clarity about a situation marked by inconsistency and bewildering shifts of attitude and feeling within the other characters. Dowell is both antithesis and reflection of Edward Ashburnham, for instance, who is at once a womanizer and an idealizer of female virtue or of Leonora, whose strict Irish Catholic morality (English-style) does not prevent her from effectively pimping for her husband. The contradictions and anomalies in the presented world require at once a moral sloth and a defective emotional life in the narrator, so that there will be no interference with his powers of observation. After Florence's death, Dowell falls into a cataleptic state, a condition that doesn't prevent him from having impressions, nor from comparing Edward's talk to that of a novelist, whose business is "to make you see things clearly" (109). Dowell has the "aloof" view that Ford says in his book on *The English Novel* is the ideal towards which the novel aspires. Writing in *The Good Soldier* is the cold instrument by which the chaos of life can be experienced as vivid impression.

In an interesting essay on "Character in *The Good Soldier*," Michael Levenson argues that in creating the "nullity" of Dowell, Ford "imagines a region of character, not only before knowledge but before desire."[3] Of course, such a character is no character at all. Levenson's characterization, as he himself acknowledges, is a useful hyperbole, suggesting a condition which Dowell approaches, but no human being could realize. Though Dowell evinces on numerous occasions evidences of desire and knowledge, it is the tendency toward "nullity" or *accidia* defines him.

Levenson explains Dowell's nullity as a function of Ford's

"method of Impressionism," which entails the "pursuit of immediate experience, the attempt to render an aboriginal stratum of personality that exists before doing, feeling and knowing take shape." He then draws the conclusion that, in his incapacity, "in an utterly improbable way Dowell becomes a compelling image of a free man. His deprivation coincides with his freedom. Dowell, the true man without qualities, can choose any qualities. Few readers will accept his assertion that Ashburnham was 'just myself,' and yet no reader can prevent the claim. Dowell cannot *be* Ashburnham, but he is extravagantly free to say so."[4]

It would seem to follow from this curious turn in the argument (though Levenson himself does not follow through) that Dowell is free to invent and reinvent the characters he presents. Such a conclusion would make nonsense of the doctrine of Impressionism, which is after all an extension of the doctrine of realism. Ford shared with Conrad the obligation "to make you see things clearly," and not things that the novelist or his surrogates are free to invent and reinvent. Dowell's "nullity" is *constrained* by the world and historical moment in which he lives. The truth of Dowell's condition is that he is *not* free to discover nor to configure patterns of character and experience, which would make life intelligible and meaningful to him. Dowell's continual bewilderment imprisons and paralyzes him.

But Levenson has perceived what seems to me an essential quality, which enhances Dowell's vision of the world. Prior to knowledge and desire, Dowell's innocence enables him to register without understanding, that is, without distortion, the desire and knowledge that exist in the world.

Dowell's narration confounds a distinction on which knowledge is based—that between illusion and reality. Thus the four together danced a minuet and behaved as a unanimity for nine long seasons. Is this a lie, a mere deception? Dowell equivocates: "it wasn't a minuet . . . it was a prison, a prison full of screaming hysterics" (7). But immediately afterward, almost in the same breath, Dowell swears by his creator, that "it was true sunshine; the true music." And isn't it true that the reader of the novel hears both the screaming hysterics and the music? The narration does not demystify the minuet, for demystification is based on a hierarchy of illusion and reality, and the hierarchy no longer exists.

82

The vexing question about Dowell's reliability is misleading, since the narration subverts the distinction between the reliable and the unreliable. Reliable narration assumes an identity or continuity between novelist and narrator; unreliable narration assumes a discrepancy between them. If Dowell is unreliable, he is not to be distinguished from the novelist's consciousness. However inconsistent we may find Dowell, there is no truth beyond the truth that he sees, no standards beyond those which he himself provides to judge shifts in consciousness and attitude. The narrator's consciousness is coterminous with the novelist's consciousness. Ford knows no more about his characters than does Dowell. The sudden bewildering shifts in tone, the oscillating judgments or feelings have no transcendent resolution in the author's consciousness. The narrative perspective is a virtual parody of the Negative Capability. Dowell sees with an empathetic selflessness that leaves him at the mercy of events. His uncertainty, bewilderment, skepticism and solipsism represent a view that only the reader can transcend, if indeed he can transcend it. Narrator and author are equally helpless before the scene they survey.

Thomas Moser's recent interpretation reveals the sources of the novel in Ford's life. Florence and Leonora correspond to Violet Hunt and his first wife, Elsie Hueffer, respectively, and the curious and distorted ways they are seen by Dowell correspond to Ford's own views of Violet and Elsie.[5] But reduction of the novel to autobiography threatens the integrity of the novel. The distinction of *The Good Soldier* is in its objectification of the quandaries of character and sexuality that Ford as well as many of his contemporaries found themselves in just before World War I.

For all the appreciative criticism of *The Good Soldier,* readers have not, in my view, sufficiently appreciated Ford's contribution to the de-authorizing tendency in modern fiction. Ford exercises his extraordinary technical skill in *The Good Soldier* less in the interest of form than in the interest of making us see vividly the uncertainty of our sexual and moral lives. Since he cannot bring his characters forward in action and dialogue in an unmediated way (for that would imply the accessible knowledge that the epistemology of the novel denies), he entrusts the narration to a highly conscious, highly articulate character whose main concern is to allow the other characters to be formed through his narration. It is a remarkable anomaly that the characters speak so little in the novel (there is, for instance, very little direct evidence that Edward Ashburnham is the great talker Dowell says he is) and yet are so vividly present. All that is possible in the way of knowledge of the others are Dowell's impressions as we have them, so the novelist is obliged to create the most vivid register of impressions, a role that Dowell performs perfectly.[6]

What is the reason for the radical unknowability of this world to even a clear-eyed observer? If he is the cold disinterested eye or, conversely, the non-personality capable of entering empathetically into the lives of others, why should he be so ignorant of their hearts? Dowell offers a reason in the first paragraph, but it is a reason that does not finally illuminate and satisfy. He attributes his ignorance to English character. Does he mean that the English are more concealed or repressed than Americans? On the evidence of Dowell's character and that of his wife, both Americans, that would hardly seem the case. Compared with Dowell and Florence, Edward and even Leonora Ashburnham wear their hearts on their sleeves. Or is it an American obtuseness in the presence of the English, Dowell never having learned to read English character accurately? There is considerable evidence of Dowell's obtuseness, most notably, his failure to perceive that his wife had been deceiving him from the very beginning of their relationship. But I do not think the obtuseness depends heavily on cultural difference. I want to suggest that Dowell's ignorance is a mimesis of the darkness that shrouds all motive, that character, as the novel understands it, is beyond knowing, not simply because it is radically unknowable, but because its very existence is in doubt. Dowell's ignorance is not an aspect of his unreliability as a narrator, because reliability of perception and knowledge is no longer possible in the world of *The Good Soldier.* Without reliability, there can be no unreliability.

Dowell understands his own ignorance as an expression of a universal condition. "Who in this world knows anything of any other heart—or of his own?" And the reason is that "one cannot be certain of the way any man will behave in any case." Lacking that certainty, the very idea of " 'character' is of no use to anyone" (155). Dowell illustrates the difficulty in his speculation about the Kilsyte case, in which Edward Ashburnham gives a weeping young girl a kiss to comfort her for the loss of her lover. At the moment, Edward's thoughts were purely paternal and consoling. But during the trial in which he was accused of a darker motive, "it came suddenly into his head whilst he was in the witness box . . . the recollection of the softness of the girl's body as he had pressed her to him. And from that moment, that girl appeared desirable to him —and Leonora completely unattractive" (156–57). Character disappears when behavior is at the mercy of the unsuspected motive, the stray impulse, the sudden accession of passion. Since character is the intelligibility of the self, how can anyone know another person if character has dissolved into a welter of motive, impulse, and passion? (Even Leonora, whose normality and conventional virtue are stressed throughout the novel is, in time of crisis, "incapable of taking any line whatever.")[7] The extraordinary shifts in point of view, often bewildering, are not signs of obtuseness or stupidity in Dowell. On the contrary, they correspond to the shifting nature of the characters themselves.[8]

The stray impulse, the unsuspected motive has always informed human behavior. Why should it now present such a gnomic aspect? The answer to this question is cultural. Dowell himself sets the cultural scene early in his narrative:

> You may well ask why I write. And yet my reasons are many. For it is not unusual in human beings who have witnessed the sack of a city or the falling to pieces of a people to desire to set down what they have witnessed for the benefit of unknown heirs or of generations infinitely remote; or, if you please, just to get the sight out of their heads.
>
> Someone has said that the death of a mouse from cancer is the whole sack of Rome by the Goths, and I swear to you that the breaking up of our little four-square coterie was such another unthinkable event. (5)

In the past civilization had erected conventions and traditions as more or less successful bulwarks against the unexpected threat from both within and without. The conventions and traditions become internalized in the virtues that compose a character. *The Good Soldier* is a story of the breakdown of internal standards of behavior and the confusion of civilized values.

The focus of the breakdown and confusion is the most difficult of all moralities, sexual morality. Early on Leonora, the continually betrayed and "virtuous" wife of Ashburnham confesses that she once tried and failed to take a lover. "And I burst out crying and I cried and I cried for the whole eleven miles. Just imagine me crying. And just imagine me making a fool of the poor dear chap like that. It certainly wasn't playing the game, was it now?" Dowell wonders whether the last remark is that "of a harlot," or what every decent woman "thinks at the bottom of her heart?" (9). Characteristically, he can't answer the question; nor does he believe that anyone can. He then formulates the problem of civilization in the grand manner of the cultural critic and moralist:

> Yet, if one doesn't know at this hour and day, at this pitch of civilization to which we have attained, after all the preachings of all the moralists. . . .
> And if one doesn't know as much as that about the first thing in the world, what does one know and why is one here? (10)

The convention that regulates marital chastity cannot be automatically invoked, because it is often purchased at the price of genuine feeling. (Edward, the man of strong sexual feeling, cannot find satisfaction in a wife whom he admires [or hates], but cannot love.) This insoluble conflict has become a banality of our sexual existence. Ford began writing the book on December 17, 1913 and the most important date in the book is August 4, the day Florence was born, began her affair with Jimmy, married Dowell, began her affair with Edward, and committed suicide. It is also the day (August 4, 1914) that England entered World War I, the day that modern life began for England. The novel, in modernist fashion, subverts the conventional understandings of Victorian and Edwardian England. Ford questions the verbal foundations of the conventions. "And that was quite in the early days of her discovery of his infidelities—if you like to call them infidelities" (56). If they are not infidelities, what are they, acts that imply a new kind of fidelity to the promptings of one's heart? But the novel does not mean to sentimentalize infidelity, since it offers a dubious picture of Edward's "sliding" heart (as in the instance of the Kilsyte case).[9]

When Dowell suggests that his story has a happy ending ("the villains—for obviously Edward and the girl were villains—have

been punished by suicide and madness. The heroine—the perfectly normal, virtuous, and slightly deceitful heroine—has become the happy wife . . .") (252), he is exercising an unstable
irony which permits us to hear a possible grain of truth in the
statement. Edward's character, like every other issue in the novel,
is unfathomable.

Sondra Stang makes an extremely suggestive connection between *The Good Soldier* and the two late essays of Freud, *Beyond
the Pleasure Principle* and *Civilization and Its Discontents*, published respectively five and fifteen years after *The Good Soldier*.
On Stang's reading, the novel explores the repressions of spirit and
passion inflicted by civilization on characters who have lived at the
pitch of civilization. Though she does not hold Dowell in high
esteem (she speaks of him as a *faux-naïf*, a narrator in bad faith),
she does credit him with raising the fundamental Freudian questions.

> Why do men find it impossible to be happy? How can they
> live if they are not to deny their instincts? What, in that case, are
> they to do with their instincts. What are they to do with the
> demands that civilization makes of them and the ways it codifies
> those demands and regulates human relationships? Given the
> nature of their natures, how can men work out ways of dealing
> with the world outside them—and the world they make? How
> much do men gain from civilization, and what in turn must they
> give up for it? What is civilization worth—how much suffering?
>
> In short, how can men find a workable relationship between
> their instincts and civilized life?[10]

Edward's tragedy is the "extinction of a splendid personality, like
the fall of a great civilization."[11] He betrays himself in "the atrophy of sexual power through disuse and paralysis. Edward has
compartmented his sexual life."[12] And Leonora "the normal type"
with little passionate energy to repress survives through her commitment to convention and tradition.

Stang's reading, which is much richer than these remarks con-
vey, is extremely suggestive, but it places the novel in a moral
framework that does not quite suit even the essays of Freud.[13]
Stang is fully alive to the extraordinary inconsistency of statement
and overstatement, of tones and attitudes in Dowell's narration,
but she is apparently unwilling to accept the inconsistencies and

contradictions as ultimate data. She tries to resolve the irreducible ambiguities of the novel. Edward's passions are, after all, themselves the product of a civilization based on traditions and conventions of honor, which account for the split within him between the idealization of women and sexual promiscuity. The split is the source of guilt, which produces a recoil from sexuality (in his passionate desire for Nancy). Does this represent the atrophy of sexual power and paralysis? I think that to formulate the question in this way is to misrepresent Edward's predicament.

In *The Good Soldier*, sexuality is a force that both generates disorder and creates new forms of deception. There are the deceptions of a society that denies the existence of sexuality, and there are also the deceptions of sexuality itself (for instance, in the behavior of Edward as well as of Florence). Ford (in *The Good Soldier*) is no advocate of free sexual expression. Dowell understands the price paid for its expression as well as for its repression. We are made witness to the sudden release of repressed energy in the modern world, which what used to be called character can no longer master. The problem is not the satisfaction of desire but rather the mastery of unsatisfied desire.

Michael Levenson describes a paradox in the novel. It would appear that passion is the enemy of understanding, that it is

> an affront to intelligibility; it not only violates the "rules" which convention lays down; it challenges the very possibilities of rules that might govern human behavior; it is not simply that characters must choose between passion and convention; it is that character begins to lose integrity as a concept.[14]

But then later in the essay he argues that "desire becomes routine and predictable—as much a matter of knowledge as of sensation."[15] It is certainly true that Ashburnham, Florence, Leonora, and Dowell himself can be seen as enacting patterns, almost compulsively, that distinguish them one from the other. But those patterns are not yet the stuff of knowledge in the novel; or, perhaps more accurately, they constitute an incipient knowledge not fully mastered. The characters in the novel, including Dowell, are victimized by ignorance of the patterns.[16]

In an extended excursus, Dowell evokes with a moving eloquence peculiar to him the nature of passion (in this case, Edward's) as a desire that includes but transcends sex, a desire for identity with the beloved, a desire for courage, for support.

> . . . if such a passion comes to fruition, the man will get what he wants. He will get the moral support, the encouragement, the relief from the sense of loneliness, the assurance of his own worth. But these things pass away as the shadows pass across sun-dials. It is sad, but it is so. The pages of the book will become familiar; the beautiful corner of the road will have turned too many times. Well, this is the saddest story. (115)

The tragedy of desire then is in the ephemeral character of the rare moments of satisfaction. The pathos of desire is that people rarely, if ever, have "what they want." Paradisal longings only intensify the overwhelming sense of life as "broken, tumultuous, agonized . . . periods punctuated by screams, by imbecilities, by deaths, by agonies" (238). It is not the repression of passion that makes for unhappiness, but the expression of passion that makes for the most intense happiness for the moment and for the deepest sadness, for it too must pass. Dowell here sounds the note not of Freud, but of Ecclesiastes.[17]

The world of *The Good Soldier* is filled with talk about religion, and it is godforsaken. Religion is seen as a cultural characteristic and as a source of neurosis. Irish Catholics in England and America lead lives quite different from the untidy lives of Mediterranean Catholics. It is impossible to disentangle Leonora's Irish Catholicism from her sexual frigidity. On the other hand, in Edward the religious sentiment has power rarely found in the English novel. In one of the most moving scenes in the novel, Dowell discovers Edward in a tormented state before an image of the Virgin Mary, praying for strength to resist the temptation of Nancy Rufford. For Edward, she is not simply an object of sexual love: she has come to be identified in his mind with the image of the Virgin herself. Edward's death seems like a martyrdom, though it is difficult to say precisely what he is a martyr to.

> [Edward] was kneeling beside his bed with his head hidden in the counterpane. His arms, outstretched, held out before him a little image of the blessed virgin—a tawdry, scarlet and Prussian-blue affair that the girl had given him on her first return from the convent. His shoulders heaved convulsively three times, and

heavy sobs came from him before she could close the door. He was not a Catholic; but that is the way it took him. (133–34)

What one senses is that the novel expresses a yearning for the religious life and a regret at its passing, because religion is the medium for soul-making. Perhaps that is what Dowell means when he responds to Leonora's declaration that she is "an Irish Catholic" after Florence had offended her: "Those words gave me the greatest relief that I have ever had in my life. They told me, I think, almost more that I have ever gathered at any one moment about myself" (46).

What is the significance of Edward's religious longing? One can only speculate. The lives of Ford's characters are defined by sexual desire or the absence of it. Edward, of course, is the central figure, the man of passion, the legatee of the nineteenth-century tragic heroines of passion, Emma Bovary and Anna Karenina. Florence, Leonora, and Dowell are reflections, as it were, of Edward's passion. Florence exhibits harlotry; Leonora, the failed desire, which then conceals itself as virtue; and Dowell impotence. Dowell is the failed essence of Ashburnham ("For I can't conceal from myself the fact that I loved Edward Ashburnham—and that I love him because he was just myself") (253). Edward moves obsessively from woman to woman finding only temporary satisfaction but no fulfillment. Indeed, if fulfillment comes to him, it is ironically, perversely, through the inhibition of his desire for Nancy, whom he imagines as an object of Christian worship. If desire cannot be satisfied, then perhaps it can be treated as a spiritual disease and be cured. The traditional cure is religious self-denial, inspired by *agape* or *philia* or *caritas*.

Edward at the end attempts to reenact Dante's love for Beatrice in his relationship with Nancy. But there is something of parody in the rendering of the relationship between Edward and Nancy, who appears in Dowell's bewildered narrative as innocent, cruel executioner, and crazed sufferer. It is as if Edward through his suicide (a mortal sin in the Catholic Church) acknowledges the futility, the absurd impossibility of the religious dispensation in the modern world. In *The Good Soldier*, desire has become an abstract, desublimated energy without object or with objects that inevitably fail to satisfy. But the failure does not sap desire of its strength; it increases its destructive power. Religion is the failed nostalgia for a sublimated desire.

There is a connection between the desublimated desire of Dowell's world and his impressionism. Dowell's experience of character and situation is disintegrated. A character never appears as a whole. "A turn of the eyebrow, a tone of the voice, a queer characteristic gesture—all these things, and it is these things that cause to arise the passion of love—all these things are like so many objects on the horizon of the landscape that tempt a man to walk beyond the horizon, to explore." And in characterizing the sexual instinct, Dowell tells us that "it can be aroused by such nothings —by an untied shoelace, by a glance of the eye in passing, etc." (114). Each impression ("a turn of the eyebrow," "a tone of voice," etc.) is a potential fetishistic object, a projection of an obsession in which the lover concentrates and by concentrating distorts his energies. Desire, a particular desire, paradoxically becomes abstract and reified.

Toward the end of the novel, Dowell asks in despair why the world is "queer and fantastic. . . . Why can't people have what they want? The things were all there to content everybody; yet everybody has the wrong thing" (237). Characteristically, he complains that he can't "make head or tail of it," and invites the reader to try. Dowell's mistake is that he assumes against the evidence of his own narrative that he knows or rather that the various characters know what they want. "Leonora wanted Edward, and she has got Rodney Bayham, a pleasant enough sort of sheep. Florence wanted Branshaw, and it is I who have bought it from Leonora. I didn't really want it; what I wanted mostly was to cease being a nurse-attendant. Well, I am a nurse-attendant. Edward wanted Nancy Rufford and I have got her." But the truth is that "want" or desire in the novel is in constant flux: and it is not simply that desires change, they can disappear as quickly as they appear.

What does it mean to say that Leonora wants Edward—how and on what terms? Leonora's cold nature makes her desire for the passionate Edward something of a puzzle. Throughout the novel, she seems to require the presence of other women to satisfy desires in Edward that she is incapable of satisfying. Florence's desire for Edward is apparent, but it is so little understood. And the complexity of Edward's relationship to Nancy (Nancy becomes an occasion in Edward for the transcendence of desire) makes Dowell's reduction of it a mark of his obtuseness. The problem is not unsatisfied desire, but the "liberation" of desire from its social and religious sublimations, its interconnections with other human energies. Desire has become rootless, alienated, the only occupation for men and women. Dowell admits to having "no attachments" (21), "nothing in the world to do" (22), "no occupations" (78). The other characters are occupied by their passions; Dowell is distinguished from the others by his lack of passion. Without work, family, national attachment, they are, however, all without occupations. Something might be said for their religious character, but the religious perspective condemns the world of *The Good Soldier*. Dowell, the cuckold, feels himself to be in limbo. And Edward and Florence are "poor wretches creeping over this earth in the shadow of an eternal wrath." Dowell's vision is Dantesque:

> But upon an immense plain, suspended in mid-air, I seem to see three figures, two of them clasped close in an intense embrace, and one intolerably solitary. It is in black and white, my picture of that judgment, an etching, perhaps; only I cannot tell an etching from a photographic reproduction. And the immense plain is the hand of God, stretching out for miles and miles, with great spaces above it and below it. And they are in the sight of God, and it is Florence that is alone. (70)

The process of disintegration is terminal: there is no rebirth. And yet the world has not fallen so far that its creatures do not know what redemption means. Dowell, after all, can conceive the Day of Judgment, and he attests to Nancy Rufford's innocence, who asks whether marriages are not sacraments (220). We have already seen that Dowell imagines the possibility of an integral love, "for identity with the woman that he loves."

> He desires to see with the same eyes, to touch with the same sense of touch, to hear with the same ears, to lose his identity, to be enveloped, to be supported. For, whatever may be said of the relation of the sexes, there is no man who loves a woman that does not desire to come to her for renewal of his courage, for the cutting asunder of his difficulties. And that will be the mainspring of his desire for her. We are all so afraid, we are all so alone, we all so need from the outside the assurance of our own worthiness to exist. (115)

Dowell believes that "if such a passion come to fruition," it too will pass. And not simply because everything passes, but because (and I am not sure what Dowell knows in this respect) this ideal of fulfillment is the projection of a fear of isolation, a futile fantasy of utter dependence on another.

The Good Soldier is a story whose vividness and intensity exceed its meaning—or lack thereof. Ford's famous commitment to Impressionism is a statement that we have nothing but impressions. Yet the impressions bespeak not an emptiness but a palpable absence. There are no longer any substantial invisibilities, only insubstantial visibilities. All permanent, meaningful structures (God, character, the virtues) have disappeared, but not the desire for them. The poignant paradox of the novel is that the aloof narrator, faithful to the surfaces of life, is a mute witness to what he cannot see and cannot know: the god that has abandoned men to their self-destructive devices. Dowell's refrain that he knows nothing expresses a humility that has an almost evangelical conviction. "I don't know what anyone has to be proud of" (52). Dowell silently chastises the pride of Leonora's Powys connection as the narrative itself chastises the pride of every character in it.

The Good Soldier is not Ford's final word. The tetralogy *Parade's End* has as its hero a character whose moral passion and integrity approach saintliness. Like Edward Ashburnham, Christopher Tietjens is a type of eighteenth-century aristocrat for whom honor is deeper than life, but unlike Edward he is not prone to inconstancy. He is a man of integrity whose actions constitute a series of refusals. He refuses to divorce his wife, though she has been unfaithful to him, because she is the mother of his child. Whether the child is his or his wife's lover's is uncertain, but it does not alter the case. He refuses to take money from his brother Mark and from his father, because his father committed suicide, believing that Tietjens had sold his wife. He refuses to turn in his friend Macmaster, who has plagiarized his research in order to gain advancement. And finally, he refuses to have an affair with Valentine Wannop out of respect for her chastity.

Tietjens is a reinvention of Edward Ashburnham, an integrity susceptible to every temptation. Tietjens is an appearance who never betrays his reality. But he is as ineffectual as Edward. "A fabulous monster," his resentful wife justly characterizes him. His refusals demonstrate a negative desire to live the life of Christ by a rejection of the world, in which every gift and power he possesses is abandoned. ("It was a condemnation of a civilization that he, Tietjens, possessed of enormous physical strength, should never have needed it before.")[18]

The narrative (there is no authorial narrator) fully acknowledges the futility of Tietjens' character through its various perspectives, but it also cherishes his idealism. It is as if Ford wishes to secure himself against the emerging nihilist "truth" that he or his narrator Dowell had discovered in *The Good Soldier:* that every "value" is a lie or, if not a lie, susceptible to betrayal by some force that contradicts it. (Edward Ashburnham, the aristocratic man of honor, lives a life of lechery, aborted by a self-destructive Dantean passion for a Beatrice-like girl.) In Tietjens, Ford invents a fabulous monster out of his own ineffectual moral yearning, against the evidence of his novelistic clearsightedness. In *Parade's End* he rewrote the saddest story.

5. Family, Incest, and Transcendence in Brontë's *Wuthering Heights*

In the works of Dostoevsky, Conrad, Mann, and Ford, we are given men who are alienated from society and family. The underground man is estranged from all human relationships. Kurtz chooses to become a god among men, and even Marlow achieves or aspires to achieve the autonomy of Buddha. Aschenbach, with a perverse willfulness, ends up a celibate, dying at a distance from the object of his desire. Ford's impotent narrator reveals himself incapable of becoming lover, husband, or father. Of the classic modernists we have considered, Lawrence alone portrays families. In this respect, he continues the tradition of the Victorian novel in which the self emerges from a matrix of family relationships. A modern character, estranged from the modern world, Ursula is the creation of the Brangwen family, of an earlier agrarian world. Yet in Lawrence's work, the repressive modalities of the world, whether pre-modern or modern, are concentrated in the Oedipal model:

the family, as we know it (not as Lawrence might ideally imagine it), remains the villain. In the major novels, *Sons and Lovers, The Rainbow,* and *Women in Love,* Lawrence dramatizes the psychic costs of familial life, providing a rationale for the development of autonomous "modern" characters.

We continue to be under the influence of the romantic ideal of individual autonomy, though at times we call it alienation. Fulfillment comes at the expense of traditional notions of family and society. Society and its microcosm, the family, in particular the bourgeois family, continue to be the objects of a profound hostility, the irreconcilable enemies of individual desire. Consider, for instance, the attack upon the family by Tony Tanner in *Adultery in the Novel.* Tanner presents adultery as a life-giving transgressive energy that subverts the "ideal aim of the bourgeois family, as of bourgeois society [which is] simply to maintain the structure it has established, to rescue it from the contingency of its origins and invest it with permanence and thus to participate in society's myth of its own perenniality."[1] If Tanner's judgment bears upon the bourgeois, he is certainly right to speak of the historical contingency of its origins, but if it is meant to encompass family as well, he is at odds with anthropological knowledge. The proclivity for familial life represents something like a natural human impulse, however varied family structures may be.

Even if one grants the cultural and historical uniqueness of the bourgeois family, Tanner's view of its imaginative possibilities seems to be distorted by ideological animus. He characterizes it as an incorrigible upholder of the status quo, resistant to change. Bourgeois discourse represses all talk that signifies desire. "Talk might be about furnishing, decoration, clothes, entertaining . . . participat[ing] in the repetition of maintenance and routine." All male talk of "business or the factory" is to be excluded.[2] It is not clear whether Tanner means to exclude the bourgeois novel from this extraordinarily confident stereotype of what is or is not available to conversation within the bourgeois family. By his own account, "the novel, in its origin, might almost be said to be a transgressive mode, inasmuch as it seemed to break, or mix, or adulterate the existing genre-expectations of the time."[3] And he clearly means to implicate the transgressive character of adultery in what he calls "the narrational urge of the novel."

It would be an easy enough task to show that conversation within the family in the bourgeois novel (see, for instance, Elizabeth Gaskell's *North and South*) is filled not only with talk of "business or factory," but also with the extraordinary dynamism of capitalist life in the nineteenth century of which the bourgeois family was at once expression and antidote. In Tanner's own account of *Madame Bovary*, for example, the urge to adultery is in part excited by the energies at play in a dynamic capitalist economy.

But Emily Brontë's *Wuthering Heights* is an even more powerful counterexample to Tanner's thesis. The incestuous passion of Heathcliff and Catherine is at once an adulterous and a familial passion. It is as if the novel revealed the passional structure or inspiration of family life. Passion at once draws its energy from familial relations and transgresses against it.

Indeed, Tanner concedes as much, though it does not seem to affect his view of the bourgeois family as a repressive structure. He adduces Rousseau's *La Nouvelle Heloise*, Goethe's *Elective Affinities*, and Flaubert's *Madame Bovary* as novels in which the family is ubiquitous. Tanner goes on to remark that "when a society ceases to care much about marriage, and all that is implied in that transaction, by the same token it will lose contact with the sense of intense passion. A novel like John Updike's *Couples* is as little about passion as it is about marriage: the adulteries are merely formal and technical. Adultery, we may say, no longer signifies."[4] Tanner here implies an equivalence between adultery and passion. Moreover, it is not simply that adulterous passion, indeed passion itself, is in opposition to marriage and family, but that marriage and family are, as it were, a breeding ground of the passionate life.

I would like to look back at *Wuthering Heights,* a premodern novel, because its extraordinary ambiguity casts light on the modern career of desire as the modern novels with their weak imagination of family life do not. *Wuthering Heights* has also been offered by certain recent modernist critics as representing both the costs of repression and a dream of the liberation of desire. *Wuthering Heights* has always been considered a sport in the history of the novel (not necessarily for good reasons). Its uniqueness and power are such that placing it within the tradition of the nineteenth-century English novel would seem to diminish it. Indeed, the novel speaks to us now with a kind of urgency that justifies, I think, the break in the historical decorum of my discussion of modernist works. *Wuthering Heights* has become very much part of the postmodern discourse of desire.

Leo Bersani's provocative and influential essay on *Wuthering Heights* focuses on the repressive character of family. He speaks of the subversion of individuality in family relationships, of "claustrophobic inbreeding" and of generational repression that denies uniqueness. According to Bersani, the family with its heterosexual norms, its commitment to its own perpetuation through procreation, is hostile to the polymorphously perverse, that is, to fragmented, discontinuous, centrifugal desire.[5] In a similar spirit, Sandra Gilbert and Susan Gubar stress the patriarchal character of family tyranny in the novel.[6] It is the Linton family that represents male tyranny, though the Lintons mask it through gentleness. (Nelly Dean in one of her more perceptive moments remarks: "Well, we *must* be for ourselves in the long run; the mild and generous are only more justly selfish than the domineering. . . .")* On this reading, Catherine is the rebellious feminine heroine and Heathcliff is her whip. Catherine (Emily's surrogate) appropriates the male strengths of the Byronic hero to affirm feminine individuality and independence against male tyranny. Bersani, Gilbert, and Gubar (among others) read the novel as an anticipation of the contemporary rebellion against the patriarchal family.[7]

Bersani, for all the penetration of his critical observations, is an ideologue of desire; literary criticism is his medium. When he says that the second part of the novel—the part defined by the relationship between the younger Catherine and Hareton—is "boring," he reveals his own modernist bias against the conditions of ordinary familial and social life that necessitates limitation, if not repression. When he denies a real connection between the two generations (saying that given the narrative outcome, Heathcliff is an "irrelevant parenthesis"),[8] he is denying (repressing?) the continuities and modulations of energy in the novel, the fact, for instance, that Heathcliff passes on the aura of energy to Hareton, confirmed by Hareton's show of filial affection for Heathcliff as the only genuine mourner of his death. Bersani's denial of a real

---

* Emily Brontë, *Wuthering Heights* (1847) (Boston: Houghton Mifflin, 1956), p. 78. All subsequent references are in the text.

connection between the generations is not a matter of interpretation but of ideological resistance to the conditions of limitation
necessary to the marriage of the younger Catherine and Hareton
and the restoration of the houses. Moreover, the denial of continuity between the generations diverts us from the familial conception of desire that unites them.

This is not to say that there is no imagination of rebellion, no
fantasy of what we now call "liberation" at work in the novel; it is
rather to draw attention to its ambiguity. If the family is a repressive structure, it also provides the "categories" of and energy for
rebellion. The ambiguity discloses itself most graphically in the
incestuous relationships in the novel. Indeed, many of the cruxes
of *Wuthering Heights* seem to converge on the incest motif. The
profound ambiguity of Emily Brontë's incestuous imagination has
baffled critics, producing in even the most intelligent among them
an incoherent response.

Thus Dorothy Van Ghent begins her interesting essay on
Wuthering Heights with a warning that the novel is the most
treacherous of all English novels "for the analytic understanding
to approach." And she attributes its treacherousness to the fact
that "it works at a level of experience that is unsympathetic to, or
rather simply irrelevant to the social or moral reason."[9] As hard as
she tries, Van Ghent does not heed her own warning. Committed
as she is to "the social and moral reason," her interpretation of the
novel is betrayed into incoherence as she approaches the "level of
experience" on which the imagination of the novel works. And the
incoherence shows itself most egregiously in her understanding of
the incest theme.

"Incest" is not a word to be found in the novel, nor is it an
object of conscious reflection as it is, say, in the novels of Faulkner
or in Gabriel Garcia Marquez's *One Hundred Years of Solitude*,
but the incest theme penetrates deeply into the imaginative matrix
of *Wuthering Heights*. Three of the most important relationships
in the novel have an unmistakable incestuous component. The
younger Catherine marries her two cousins, and though Heathcliff
and the elder Cathy are only foster brother and sister, there is
between them the greatest identity of "kind," as Van Ghent aptly
remarks. For Van Ghent, incest is a condition destructive to individuality *and* relationship. "Impassioned by their brother-and-

sisterlike identity of kind Heathcliff and Catherine can only destroy each other, for it is impossible for two persons to be each
other (as Catherine says she 'is' Heathcliff) without destruction of
the physical limitations that individualize and separate." Incest
figures again destructively in the relationship between the younger
Catherine and Linton Heathcliff: "the implicit incestuousness of
the 'two children figure' is suggested morbidly by Linton's disease
and by his finally becoming a husband only as a corpse." Even the
prospectively successful marriage of Catherine and Hareton is
achieved only by what Van Ghent calls "symbolic emasculation,"
the influence of "Victorian ameliorism." "Cathy literally teaches
the devil out of Hareton and 'esteem' between them takes the place
of the old passion for identification." Van Ghent implicitly suggests an equivalence between the incestuous and the demonic—or
at least that the exorcising of the one is the exorcising of the other.
What is lost, Van Ghent goes on to say, is "the great magic, the
wild power, of the original two," Heathcliff and Catherine.[10]

But does the incest motive make for destruction in *Wuthering
Heights?* Van Ghent's civilized abhorrence of incest causes her to
misread all three relationships. Thus, for example, she misrepre-
sents the facts about Linton Heathcliff. Linton's delicate health
can hardly be a psychosomatic expression of the incestuous atmo-
sphere of this relationship to Catherine, since it is a fact before he
even meets her. His meeting with her, rather than hastening his
death, prolongs his life. Indeed, we are invited to believe that
Catherine Linton's vitality may be his salvation. Linton is the
"inconceivable" child of aversion and hatred, the product of the
nonincestuous marriage between Heathcliff and Isabella Linton.
The relationship between Catherine and Hareton succeeds where
the earlier relationship fails precisely because of their familial connection. Heathcliff, for example, implies the connection in his
painful awareness of Hareton's resemblance to Cathy's mother.
"But, when I look for his father in his face, I find *her* every day
more!" (257). If Catherine is a softer version of her mother, less
fierce and more civilized, it is because of the Linton side of her
nature. Paradoxically, it gives her a power that her mother never
enjoyed, the power to civilize a man.

The incoherence of Van Ghent's interpretation becomes patent
when "the great magic" and "wild power" of "the original two" is

invoked as a measure of the inadequacy of the relationship between Catherine and Hareton. Earlier Van Ghent speaks of the "unnaturalness and impossibility of the mating" of Heathcliff and Catherine, implying the operation of the incest taboo and, as we have already seen, views their sense of being identical with one another as an obscene violation of the physical boundaries that separate people and make individuality possible. Van Ghent simply fails to reconcile the view of Heathcliff and Catherine as a wild and magical pair with the view of them as destructively incestuous. Her concluding tribute to "the original pair" implicitly concedes (her strictures against the incest motive notwithstanding) that the very source of their attractiveness and power lies in their incestuous dream of realizing their shared identity.

> We are led to speculate on what the bounty might have been, had the windowpane not stood between the original pair, had the golden child and the dark child not been secularized by a spelling book. Perhaps, had the ideal and impossible eventuality taken place, had the "inside" and the "outside", the bright child and the dark one, become identified in such a way that they could freely assume each other's modes, then perhaps the world of the animals and the elements—the world of wild moor and barren rock, of fierce wind and attacking beast, that is the strongest palpability in *Wuthering Heights*—would have offered itself completely to human understanding and creative intercourse. Perhaps the dark powers that exist within the soul, as well as in the outer elemental world, would have assumed the language of consciousness, or consciousness would have bravely entered into companionship with those dark powers and transliterated their language into its own.[11]

We need not speculate about the bounty, for the novel itself provides it in the symbolic consummation (in death) of Heathcliff and in the younger Cathy and Hareton.

Van Ghent perceives the vitality of the incestuous desire of Heathcliff and Catherine for each other. It is the vitality of the novel itself, but she cannot reconcile it to her moral judgment of its destructiveness and morbidity. What she fails to see, I think, is the way Brontë dissociates morbidity and destructiveness from death. Heathcliff and Cathy *die into another kind of life*. Van Ghent is, of course, right to stress the insistence on identity between Catherine and Heathcliff and its "destruction of the physical limitations that individualize and separate," but she fails to see its aim, which is not death but life, or rather life-in-death. The sentiment of a non-Christian eternal life is given to us in the concluding stanza of Brontë's poem, which begins "No coward soul is mine." "There is not room for Death / Nor atom that his might could render void / Since thou art Being and Breath / And what thou art may never be destroyed." I want to stress, however, that Emily Brontë conceives the "illimitable" desire of "the original two" as paradoxically constrained by the deepest of family relations, the blood tie. Satisfaction of desire can be achieved only by transgressing the incest taboo, whether in the spiritual or sexual sense of the phrase.

Incest is never mentioned in the novel, because it enters so deeply into the world that it is taken for granted. Catherine Linton asserts what may be the credo of the novel, the belief in the superiority of the blood tie over the marriage bond: "I should never love anybody better than papa. . . . And people hate their wives, sometimes, but not their sisters and brothers" (202). If one generously extends its meaning to include cousins and foster relationships, "incest" is an inescapable condition of all the relationships in the novel. If the young Catherine is to remain within the world of Wuthering Heights and Thrushcross Grange, she can expect to find a mate only in her cousins, young Linton and Hareton. That world is insistently xenophobic. When a stranger appears, as he does at the very beginning of the novel, all the characters of the household of Wuthering Heights, whatever their feelings for one another, conspire to exclude him. The opening episode immediately precludes the possibility of a match between Lockwood and Catherine. Lockwood's romantic pretentiousness and timidity make him utterly unsuited to Catherine, and she encounters his intrusion into the household of Wuthering Heights with a withering "scorn." But it is his alien character, not simply his peculiarity that makes Lockwood an unsuitable mate.

Much of the critical attention to Lockwood understandably focuses on his role as narrator and surrogate for the reader, who like Lockwood enters (imaginatively) into a strange world. Whatever other lesson Lockwood learns, he eventually is supposed to see the universality of the experience, not its regional peculiarity.

And certainly the violence of Lockwood's dreams early in the novel suggests that his visit to Yorkshire makes it possible for him to penetrate to a level of his own consciousness to which he has no access in the civilized life of London. But the level of experience to which Lockwood penetrates is one which values kind and excludes the stranger.

The other significant "stranger" in the novel, Heathcliff himself, is a paradoxical case.[12] An orphan, a dark child from the streets of Liverpool who has been brought into the world of Wuthering Heights by Earnshaw, the paterfamilias, he quickly establishes himself as Earnshaw's favorite to the envious disgust of his son Hindley. To account for the affection shown to him, one critic has plausibly suggested that Heathcliff may be Earnshaw's illegitimate son and hence half-brother to Catherine.[13] In any case, Wuthering Heights completely naturalizes Heathcliff. He becomes the favorite son, the true brother of Catherine, the very incarnation of the spirit of the place, its heath and cliff. The degeneration of the house corresponds to Heathcliff's exclusion by the "usurper" Hindley. (When he returns from exile to exact his revenge, Heathcliff catalyzes a process of degeneration that has already occurred with Hindley's degradation.) The lost principle of vitality that must be brought in from the outside, Heathcliff is transformed from stranger to brother. For Catherine he is never "other."

In the Catherine-Heathcliff vision of the cosmos, individuality and difference are signs of estrangement and not fulfillment. The novel aims to overcome the separations that define our conventional existence. When early in the novel, the ghost of Catherine returns to Wuthering Heights and extends her hand through the window in the room where Lockwood is drowsing, she crosses the barrier between dreaming and waking, between death and life. Lockwood's ferocious response of rubbing her wrist against the broken glass may signal an unconscious resistance to the threat that the overcoming of the barrier poses. There are good psychological reasons to want to keep separate the realms of waking and dreaming, death and life.

For Catherine, however, such a separation is anathema. Life as it is ordinarily lived becomes a prison that separates her from the authentic life on the moors where she will ultimately enjoy her identification with Heathcliff. Early in the novel, Catherine describes to Nelly a dream in which she is flung out of heaven by angry angels only to find herself on Wuthering Heights "sobbing for joy." And on her deathbed, she speaks of her conventional life as a "shattered prison" from which she hopes to escape into "that glorious world" (137). Catherine speaks the language of transcendence, but one that contrasts with the traditional transcendence of which Nelly Dean speaks. "Well might Catherine deem that heaven would be a land of exile to her, unless, with her mortal body, she cast away her mortal character also" (135). And Heathcliff has a corollary fantasy, which enables him to relinquish "the levers and mattocks" of revenge so that he can go to his death or to the greater life with Catherine. What Catherine's desire shares with Christian longing is a belief in the possibility of glory beyond the limitations and ordeals of ordinary life. It also shares with Christianity a yearning for peace and harmony, which in the Christian imagination have always given off the radiant emanation of glory. Unlike the Christian view, however, glory is to be found in a natural world in which the divisions and limitations of ordinary life are overcome. A view of the novel which stresses the destructiveness of the incestuous passions in their failure to respect "the physical limitations that individualize and separate" simply ignores the aim of overcoming limitations and separation.

For Heathcliff and Catherine, the condition of separation and difference in ordinary life is the condition of passion. Only in death can one find release from passion and gain serenity.

> I lingered round them, under that benign sky; watched the moths fluttering among the heath and hare-bells; listened to the soft wind breathing through the grass; and wondered how anyone could ever imagine unquiet slumbers, for the sleepers in that quiet earth. (287)

Thomas Moser finds irony in this passage because he cannot forget Heathcliff in exile, "perpetually vibrant with passion, and of Cathy ceaselessly haunting him."[14] He acknowledges that Emily Brontë did not perceive the irony, but he fails to say why. How could she, for she had a visionary sense, unavailable to secular and rationalist critics, of an intense and serene "life" in "death." It is as if Heathcliff and Catherine were able to sublimate their passion, divesting it of its suffering. Both Emily Brontë and her readers want to have it both ways. They are unwilling to surrender the passion, but wish for the peace that Catherine's triumphant "death" brings.

In *The Disappearance of God*, Hillis Miller provides a characterization of the narrative pattern of the novel.

> [Catherine and Heathcliff] are united in childhood, separated in adulthood, and reach union again only in the boundless realm of death. Their love moves through a process of union, separation and reunion on a triple level which appears often in writings in the romantic tradition, and is like the dialectic of Hegel or like Novalis' vision of human life and history.[15]

In *Natural Supernaturalism*, Meyer Abrams has written a cultural history of this pattern, which he understands as a secularization of the parable of the Prodigal Son.

> The Bible also contained an apt, detailed, and impressive figure for life as a circular rather than a linear journey, which had been uttered explicitly as a parable of man's sin and redemption, and by the authoritative voice of Jesus himself. This was the story of the Prodigal Son (Luke 15:11–32), who collected his inheritance and "took his journey into a far country, and there wasted his substance with riotous living"; then, remorseful, made his way back to his homeland and the house of his father, who joyously received him, clothed him in the best robe, a ring, and shoes, and ordered the fatted calf that they might "eat, and be merry; For this my son was dead, and is alive again; he was lost, and is found."[16]

The pattern in *Wuthering Heights*, however, is not a secularized substitute for the Christian drama of salvation, but an aggressively conceived alternative. The narrow and punishing Puritanism of Joseph and even the more benign piety of Nelly Dean offer prospects of eternal suffering for both Heathcliff and Catherine. Joseph and Nelly are preoccupied with sin and try unsuccessfully to instill a sense of guilt in Catherine and Heathcliff, for whom sin is irrelevant. (All attempts to induce a Christian conscience in Heathcliff are to no avail; "I tell you, I have nearly attained *my* heaven; and that of others is altogether unvalued and uncoveted by me" [283].) The "religion" of the novel is atavistically pagan, sharing with Christianity the pattern of primal unity, disrupted and regained. What distinguishes it from Christianity are the terms of the pattern and an awareness of Christianity as an agent of division and separation.

One might argue that Emily Brontë's atavistic pantheism is itself an agent of division in a Christian world. No conception of wholeness and identity can successfully totalize experience insofar as it necessarily sets itself against other conceptions. In a sense, however, the Heathcliff-Catherine dispensation does not set itself against Christianity. The great turning point in the novel is Heathcliff's relinquishing "the levers and the mattocks" (274) of revenge, his indifference to the claims of the ordinary world, which includes Christian attitude and sentiment. Christianity and civility are forms of the ordinary world that persist after Heathcliff leaves it to meet Catherine on the moors. Nelly Dean's fantasy of Catherine's "blessed release" in death suggests a possible compatibility between the Christian dream of transcendence with the "pantheistic" fulfillment of Heathcliff and Catherine.

> I see a repose that neither earth nor hell can break; and I feel an assurance of the endless and shadowless hereafter—the Eternity they have entered—where life is boundless in its duration, and love in its sympathy, and joy in its fullness. (141)

Nelly's speech anticipates the concluding vision of "the sleepers" in the quiet earth. The narrative strategy of *Wuthering Heights* with multiple perspectives (those of Lockwood, Nelly Dean, Isabella, Catherine, Heathcliff) resists any single ideological reading of the novel. What we are given is at once a contestation and a reconciliation of two moralities: the Christian and the Blakean (cum Brontëan), the morality of control and order and the morality of energy.

What role does the family play in the drama of rebellion and transcendence? If family becomes a form of tyranny, it also provides a means of escape from or transcendence of tyranny through a fantasy of "incest." The threat to the integrity of the self comes not from the family, but from the outside—that is, from the other family. The Lintons threaten the Earnshaws; the Earnshaws, the Lintons; weakness and strength are inimical. That is to say, there is a moral imperative within each family to abide by its nature—

its kind of energy and disposition. Compatibility in this world is in the "marriage," figurative as well as literal, of like-to-like (brother-to-sister, cousin-to-cousin). Edgar and Catherine, Heathcliff and Isabella, the younger Catherine and Linton Heathcliff illustrate Heathcliff's assertion of the tragic absurdity of relationships in which there are "natural" (and familial) disaffinities. "And that insipid, paltry creature [Edgar Linton] attending her from *duty* and humanity! From pity and charity he might as well plant an oak in a flowerpot and expect it to thrive, as imagine he can restore her to vigour in the soil of his shallow cares" (131). Sameness, resemblance, repetition are not negatives in Brontë's world: they are the expressions of desire. And they guarantee survival either in ordinary life or in the immortality of the natural world. Heathcliff and Catherine must escape the ordinary family bond to become a couple in a natural world that is the objective correlative of their energies. The possibility of happiness between the younger Catherine and Hareton and the restoration of their houses derives from their resemblance to each other.

Nature triumphs in both relationships. Misery and unfulfillment are functions of difference and disaffinity. The excessive energies of Heathcliff and Catherine, however impressive they may be, simply cannot be confined to any society. Their aim, by necessity, is to achieve fulfillment in a "place," call it death or nature or "the eternity of the phenomenon" (Nietzsche's phrase). Their "freedom," beyond ordinary life, lies in this necessity. What is both disturbing and confusing to readers is that God whose place in Christianity is transcendent (a place beyond) has been here inserted into both the social and natural worlds. Heathcliff and Catherine are gods or demons of immanence: Heathcliff, Catherine tells us, resembles the eternal rocks beneath. The violence is the result of an *overfilling* or *overcharging* of human and natural space with divinity. Brontë gives us an implicit critical view of the totalizing ambition of the romantic imagination. Cathy and Hareton are not tame: they have domesticated the energy of the "original two" but with an implicit reverence for that energy. In them, we experience a *human* accommodation of the energy to the cultivated space of society. The successful marriage of Catherine and Hareton depends upon the union of Heathcliff and Catherine outside the social space.

The "meaning" of the fierce passion of Heathcliff and Catherine is deeper than erotic desire, indeed is inimical to it. Catherine speaks of her love for Heathcliff as a necessity, not as a source of delight or pleasure: "—my love for Heathcliff resembles the eternal rocks beneath—a source of little visible delight, but necessary" (70). It is the suffering need for the joy and serenity of union. In saying this, I am asserting the essential chastity of the relationship, a chastity perfectly consonant with the fact that the primal unity between them is prepubescent and the unity at the end a disembodied fusion of spirits within the natural world. It is the body that makes for difference and separation and that is the source of sexual desire. Brontë's naturalism transcends or "represses" sexual desire, conceives it as a threat because of the very intensity of desire in the lovers. Desire is displaced from sexuality to a religiously resonant "spiritual," though not Christian, relationship.

Thomas Moser's ingenious speculation on the possibility that Heathcliff fathered the younger Cathy may have some basis in the time scheme of the novel, but it is a violation of the spirit of their relationship.[17] It also contradicts what the novel explicitly tells us. "She was the most winning thing that ever brought sunshine into a desolate house—a real beauty in face—with the Earnshaw's handsome dark eyes, but the Linton's fair skin, and small features, and yellow curling hair" (160). There is no provocation here to question the reliability of Nelly Dean's narration. Hillis Miller is on target. "That Heathcliff and the first Cathy should not be the parents of the second Cathy is not only necessary to the plot, but also has a meaning as a definition of their love. Their love can have no earthly fruits, but lead unequivocally to death. The essence of their love is their unwillingness to sacrifice their oneness to anything else."[18]

The desire for union may be a loss of personality in the conventional or secular sense, but in a deeper religious sense it is a desire for *identity,* a curiously ambiguous word. Estrangement entails not only loneliness, but the possible loss of one's reality, one's *identity.* Identity understood as difference from others is always threatened by dissolution. Paradoxically, who I am requires confirmation by others, or to take it a step further, realization through others. Identity becomes a sign for religious aspiration. Heathcliff and Catherine are each other's god.

Characters are described as: wolves, lambs, cats, mice, frost, fire, thunder, calm. Human life, it would seem, is one of Hobbesian brutishness, fiercely oppositional, the moments of peace ephemeral calms after the storm. Yet there is an implicit idea of alienation and estrangement to be overcome. The moral imperative is to be one with one's natural energy. Self-betrayal is doom. The family and its norms may keep one from self-fulfillment: social necessity dictates Catherine's marriage to Edgar Linton. In order for Catherine to be one with herself (that is, to experience her identity with Heathcliff), she would have to escape the confines of family, to transgress its boundaries. At the same time, the movement toward identity is inward, toward the most extreme expression of familial "integrity," the "incestuous" bond of like and like, of sister and brother. Transcendence is a movement inward, not beyond. Catherine and Heathcliff seek to recover home, the lost "glorious world" of Wuthering Heights.

In *Wuthering Heights* there is only family and the natural world: there is no society in the larger sense. Family itself is a version of nature, or families are versions of nature. As Bersani remarks, "to go from *Wuthering Heights* to the Grange is not to go from nature to society; it is to go from the strong children to the weak children, or more precisely, from aggressively selfish children to whiningly selfish children."[19] The movement of transgression and transcendence is itself determined by the familial imagination. The mutual yearning of Catherine and Heathcliff is one version of the pervasive desire of the novel, the desire for home. For Emily Brontë the ordered, closed world of nature and family is not one of freedom, but of absolute necessity. *Wuthering Heights* argues neither for nor against the authority of family. It is simply an inescapable condition of the life of the novel: for all of its explosiveness, *Wuthering Heights* remains ineluctably Victorian in this respect. But what is more significant is the novel's powerful intuition of the human need, an exigency more powerful than desire (a desire more powerful than Desire), for bonds of connection and identity with others for which we have invented no more powerful structure than the family. Our literature and philosophy have taught us that the satisfaction of desire is the return home. In a sense, however, we can't go home again. The deepest psychic and cultural prohibition is the incest

109

taboo, which forever separates us from the mother, the very incarnation of the home. With unequalled intensity in modern literature, Emily Brontë imagines desire breaking through the barrier of insatiability to an ultimate satisfaction in death. Heathcliff and Catherine achieve their fulfillment, sister and brother as lovers, passionately embracing on the site of home and family. Rather than an obstacle to desire, the family may be its very object.

Thus Juliet Mitchell, a feminist theorist, contemplating the prospect of transcending the family structure, reminds us of the "pervasiveness of familial metaphors and of the family as a vantage point in our culture." She wants the question of whether "feminist theorizing should go beyond the family" to be considered. "I believe before the familial can be transcended or left behind, all positions within the family must be probed from all directions. . . ."[20] She has already raised the question about whether family structures can or should be left behind. Mitchell argues that the stress on the importance of the nuclear family in bourgeois society in contrast to the more extended family in, for example, pre-industrial and tribal societies exacerbates rather than strengthens the incest motive.[21] Paradoxically, within a pastoral setting, *Wuthering Heights* provides us with an extraordinary example of the incestuous character of the nuclear family, what Mitchell characterizes, following Friedrich Engels, as "the holy (bestial) family."[22] The history of the modern world represents a neverending effort to discover alternative structures.

In *Wuthering Heights* the family constitutes a structure to express and contain the energies it generates. In the modern imagination, desire floats free in an indeterminate artistic or bohemian space, represented in the work of the alienated artist. "Free-floating," however, may be an illusion, for having apparently escaped the tyranny of society's demands, the artist hero may still be implicated in the regime of self in which the familial (as well as social) structures continue to be internalized and insurmountable. The deepest of all desires is the desire for home. Could it be that the paradoxical lesson to be drawn from *Wuthering Heights* is that illimitable desire which, as Proust says, like the imagination knows no bounds, seeks an origin (home, unity, identity), the ultimate bounded condition, from which the desiring subject is forever excluded? This knowledge is present in repressed form in *Remembrance of Things Past*, as we have already remarked in considering the psychoanalytic interpretation of the Proustian text. In *Wuthering Heights*, incestuous union and the journey home have been attained in the imagination.

6. Desire and Its Discontents

Writing is one of the most extraordinary achievements of conscious civilized life. It is also an amazing achievement of subconscious life. The paradox becomes intelligible once we realize that writing here has a special significance: it is a reflection of a particular strategy in a civilization to recover energies civilization is no longer conscious of, which its behavior and conventions have silenced.

In the early phase of the modern period, represented in my discussion by Proust, Dostoevsky, Conrad, Freud, Mann, Lawrence, and Ford (and these are only exemplary instances and not the only ones), the effect of the recovery of desire through writing is to reveal the dangers. The resultant wisdom is cautionary. Writing expresses and testifies to a life that cannot be truly lived or can be lived only at great peril. The lesson of classic modern fiction, however, is not without its ambiguity. If the life of the passions is terrifying, it may in part be the result of excessive repression. In *Civilization and Its Discontents,* Freud makes the argument that repression is the necessary cost of civilization, and yet excessive (unnecessary) repression may provoke a violent return of the repressed. Both Kurtz and Aschenbach exemplify such a state. In the present phase of the modern period this wisdom is challenged. Perhaps our repressive or repressed consciousness suffers from a distortion that makes desire *seem* destructive. Destructiveness or self-destructiveness may not be intrinsic to desire, but rather a product of repressive consciousness. Postmodern thought and literature represent the ambiguity I have just ascribed to the modern period as the unambiguous destructive repressiveness of civilization. I would like to sketch our recent cultural history (or a significant aspect of it) in which the writing of desire becomes a celebration of it, a utopian projection of its living realizations. Even if desire has a destructive aspect, its vitality is so congenial to the imagination (indeed its very source, in the romantic view) that it overrides whatever ethical or rational opposition one might mount against it.

The exemplary figures in this history are writers of the 1950s, Herbert Marcuse (in *Eros and Civilization,* 1955) and Norman O. Brown (in *Life Against Death,* 1959). In the fifties psychoanalysis, a revolutionary force in the decades of the twenties and the thirties, had achieved an immense conservative authority, indeed had become a way of life, a kind of secular religion for the educated middle class in the urban centers of America. Psychoanalysis became a clinical practice with all the institutional prestige of a medical science. No longer the revolutionary of the twenties, Freud came to be regarded as a master, the authority in a tradition that bears his name, comparable to Marx vis-à-vis Marxism or the church fathers vis-à-vis medieval Christianity. Disputes were resolved by appeal to the "sacred" Freudian text—or to a particular understanding of the text. The psychoanalytic orthodoxy resolved the apparently Manichean dualisms in Freud's thought—consciousness vs. unconsciousness, ego vs. id, reality vs. pleasure—on the side of the repressive term in each case. The reality principle (and its cognate terms: ego, consciousness) had been elevated to the superior place in the psychoanalytic hierarchy. The healthy psyche was now obliged to postpone its gratifications and accommodate itself to social reality. Orthodox theory and practice in effect dissolved Freud's ambivalent and equivocal view of the Manichean struggles within self and civilization.

Marcuse and Brown asserted the claims of desire, pleasure, unconsciousness against this psychoanalytic orthodoxy—indeed, against all the repressed terms in the Freudian oppositions. Marcuse openly reacted against the Enlightenment legacy in the psychoanalytic tradition. I cite again the passage: "Self-consciousness and reason, which have conquered and shaped the historical world, have done so in the image of repression, internal and external. They have worked as the agents of domination; the liberties they have brought (and these are considerable) grew in the soil of enslavement and have retained the mark of their birth."[1] (Marcuse, I think, produces a view of the Enlightenment as excessively rationalistic, in which, for instance, Hume's and Rousseau's valorizing of passions and desires have no place.) Marcuse shared with his orthodox antagonists an enormous respect for Freud's achievement. He, too, believed that Freud was the central figure of modern culture. But his intellectual development does not lie exclusively within the Freudian tradition. He came to Freud as a member of the Frankfurt school, formed on the traditions of Hegel and Marx and was primarily concerned with the political and social implications of Freudian psychological categories.

Before proceeding with a reading of Marcuse, we should pause to consider the legitimacy of a political reading of Freud, especially in the light of recent arguments that insist on the apolitical, asocial, acultural character of his thought. Thus Richard Rorty writes: "Freud . . . has no contribution to make to social theory. His domain is the portion of morality that cannot be identified with 'culture'; it is the private life, the search for a character, the attempt of individuals to be reconciled with themselves (and, in the case of some individuals, to make their lives works of art)."[2] Rorty allies himself with Phillip Rieff, who asserts "psychoanalysis is the doctrine of the private man defending himself against public encroachment"[3] in contradistinction to the political interpretations of Erich Fromm and Herbert Marcuse.

Is it plausible to divide the private from the public, social, and cultural in the work of a thinker whose central idea is the concept of repression? The political resonance of the term "repression" is not accidental. Freud himself explored analogies between psychic and social domination in *Civilization and Its Discontents*. If the self internalizes the repressive structures of civilization, then it is misleading to speak of a defense against encroachment, since civilization already possesses the so-called private man. Indeed, privacy may be the result of an attempt to mitigate what comes close to a totalitarian situation, and may even turn out to be an illusion. In its microcosmic familial form, civilization determines and shapes the very condition of privacy. Freud may have no contribution to make to social theory in the sense that he has no substantial conception of social change, since for him society is a relatively unmalleable entity, but his understanding of the self is unquestionably social.

In a different way, though to similar effect, Carl Schorske evaporates the political significance of Freud's achievement by dividing the psychological from the political. Schorske recreates the historical context of the emergence of psychoanalysis—in particular, "the power of the New Right both in Austria and abroad."[4] In a subtle analysis of Freud's four Rome dreams, Schorske shows how Freud identified Rome as "the [Christian] promised land" from which, like Moses and Hannibal, he had been forbidden access and against which he wished to avenge himself. (Schorske notes that Freud traveled to Italy between 1895 and 1898 without ever reaching Rome, as if he were held back by some inhibition which his Rome dreams reveal.) Freud's sensitivity to the anti-Semitic culture in which he lived was intensified by an anti-Semitic episode in which his father had been an acquiescent victim. "Little Sigmund was disgusted with his father's unheroic behavior." He contrasted his situation with another "which fitted my feelings better: the scene in which Hannibal's father . . . made his boy swear before the household altar to take vengeance on the Romans."[5]

Schorske argues that in accepting "the help of socially influential individuals to secure" the respectable position of professor, Freud after years of struggle released himself from "the spell of Hannibal's oath." The discovery of psychoanalysis "made it possible for Freud to overcome his Rome neurosis, to kneel at Minerva's ruined temple, and to regularize his academic status." Schorske reads the effect of Freud's achievement as the reduction of politics to an "epiphenomenal status" and in relation to "the primal conflict between father and son" a kind of evasion of political reality that could make "bearable [for liberals] a political world spun out of orbit and control."[6]

But isn't it possible to see "the primal conflict" in political terms as emblematic of the authoritarianism of the entire culture? (We read Kafka in this way.) The primal conflict, after all, acted itself out, or more accurately was repressed in the gymnasium, the workplace and the state as well as in the family. Here politics is not simply a metaphor for psychology but the reality that subsumes psychology itself. So explosive were Freud's discoveries that it seems almost obtuse to characterize them as apolitical and evasive. No authoritarian society could fail to perceive the possible threat to its authority posed by psychoanalysis. Marcuse is right to pursue the political and social implications of Freudian thought. What the implications are remains at issue.

It should be remarked apropos of Marcuse's critique of Enlightenment reason that his identification of reason with repression is based on a misconstruing of the Freudian concept of repression. As Freud stated with special emphasis in his 1915 essay on "Repression," "*the essence of repression lies simply in the function of rejecting and keeping something out of consciousness.*"[7] It need hardly be said that the essence of self-consciousness and reason is to bring something to consciousness. Indeed, the insidiousness of repression is precisely its unconscious character. I say "unconscious" rather than "irrational" because repression *has* its reasons (e.g., the reduction of pain that might be the inadvertent consequence of the satisfaction of an instinct). But the "reason" of repression is "correlated" (Freud's word) with the unconscious and not to be confused with rational consciousness. Conscious rational reflection, far from being repressive, may be a path of psychic liberation. Marcuse's idea of repression has its source not in Freud but in political theory, where repression is conscious more often than not.

Marcuse's aim (and Brown's as well) is to establish the possibility of a nonrepressive civilization. This idea, it would seem, is a contradiction in terms—in which civilization is by definition repressive. How then is such a possibility imaginable? How can civilization become the direct expression of erotic energy, a field of self-delighting aesthetic play, if the repressive character of civilization is a fundamental premise of Freudian thought? Marcuse accepts Freud's account of the repressive character of civilization, but he historicizes it, that is, he sees it as a function of a specific historical organization of society, not as intrinsic to it. Marcuse characterizes the principle behind this function as the *"performance principle:* the prevailing historical form of the *reality principle."* (The present historical form of the reality principle is bourgeois society, of which psychoanalytic orthodoxy is a particular expression.) The historicizing of civilization Marcuse believes to be an implication of Freud's own work, though it is concealed by the concept of the reality principle, which makes "historical contingencies into biological necessities." Marcuse even endorses Freud's view that "a repressive organization of the instincts underlies *all* historical forms of the reality principle in civilization," but he notes Freud's historical insight "that civilization has progressed as organized *domination."* [8] If the historical dimension were lacking, it would be futile to advocate as Freud does in *Civilization and Its Discontents* a mitigation of the severity of repression.

Marcuse never relinquishes the category of repression. Indeed, he makes a crucial distinction between basic and surplus repression, between restrictions necessitated by social domination and the " 'modifications' of the instincts necessary for the perpetuation of the human race in civilization." Nonrepressive civilization is something of an exaggeration in Marcuse's argument. The essential claim is that repression engendered by "social domination" is not a necessity of civilization. The raison d'être of social domination, Marcuse argues in Marxian fashion, relates to an economy of scarcity characterized by an acute competition for the objects of desire. Social domination is also a function of the early phase of industrialism when the economy is being transformed into one of abundance. What occurs is a paradox (a Weberian rather than Marxist insight) in which the productive conditions of industrial civilization require in the interest of efficiency the repression of the very desires fostered by the industrial revolution. The expansive sense of desire and power is given to us, for instance, in this passage from Elizabeth Gaskell's *North and South:*

> [Margaret Hale] liked the exultation in the sense of power
> which these Milton men [industrialists of the north] had. It might

be rather rampant in its display, and savour of boasting; but still they seemed to defy the old limits of possibility, in a kind of fine intoxication, caused by the recollection of what had been achieved, and what yet should be. If in her cooler moments she might not approve of their spirit in all things, still there was much to admire in their forgetfulness of themselves and the present, in their anticipated triumphs over all inanimate matter at some future time which none of them should live to see.[9]

In practice, of course, the working conditions of factory life require the regulating of this "fine intoxication." The paradoxical result is an intensification of repression as civilization multiplies desires and the possibilities of their satisfaction. Marcuse writes at a moment when the economy of abundance has outgrown its repressive origins and surplus repression is no longer an historical necessity. He envisions a democratic society of material abundance which reduces necessary labor to a minimum and frees the person to live a life of creative leisure. Such a life has been historically possible to a small privileged class: Marcuse wants to make it available to everyone. The possibility of leisure, however, is not enough. What is required now is a transformation of psychic life in which work becomes play, an erotically charged nonutilitarian activity.

In distinguishing between repression that enforces social domination and "repression" required for survival, Marcuse opens up the possibility of lifting taboos against so-called perversion. Heterosexual genital sexuality need not be the only permissible sexuality. It is, for Marcuse, gratuitously repressive of the full range of sexuality, which is by "nature" polymorphously perverse and not exclusively genital. Perversions may pose threats to social or patriarchal domination but they do not threaten survival. It is important to note that Marcuse's advocacy of the polymorphously perverse is not in the interest of a liberal tolerance for the variety of sexual expression. Polymorphous perversity is an expression of the happiness of *all*, the *promesse de bonheur*.[10]

Freud does not argue *for* polymorphous perversity, but in his rejection of perversion there is a *tendency* in the direction of advocacy.

. . . The essence of the perversions lies not in the extension of the sexual aim, not in the replacement of the genitals, not even

119

always in the variant choice of the object, but solely in the exclusiveness with which the deviations are carried out and as a result of which the sexual act serving the purpose of reproduction is put on one side.[11]

Freud does not object to the variety of erotic expression, but to the exclusiveness of its expression in one direction. Perversion and polymorphous perversity are *almost* opposites. The one form of exclusiveness that would not be condemned by Freud is genital reproductive sexuality.

The mythical origin of repression, that is, of social domination, according to Freud, is to be found in the crime of the sons against the father, the crime of patricide described in *Totem and Taboo*. The inevitable consequence of the crime is psychological guilt and the political and social enforcement of paternal authority. Marcuse's extrapolation of the Freudian argument is an attack on patriarchal domination. This argument sanctions feminism without being explicitly feminist.

It is, of course, one thing to establish the theoretical possibility of a nonrepressive civilization and of a nonrepressed self, but it is another to create such a civilization and self. The Marxist solution is not available to Marcuse. The proletariat, the agent of Marxist revolution against oppression and exploitation, cannot be expected to be an instrument of *erotic* liberation. The psychological repression described by Freud and Marcuse is endemic to the whole society; it is not confined to a specific class. What is therefore required is a psychic force to overthrow internal repression.

Marcuse's solution is aesthetic, the playful eroticizing of consciousness already anticipated in Schiller's *Letters on an Aesthetic Education*. In Schiller, "the stress is on the impulsive, instinctual character of the aesthetic function."[12] Marcuse also finds support in the aesthetics of Kant and Hegel. "The truth of art is the liberation of sensuousness through its reconciliation with reason: this is the central notion of classical idealistic aesthetics." Marcuse quotes Hegel:

> . . . thought is materialized, and matter is not extraneously determined by thought but is itself free in so far as the natural, sensuous, affectional possess their measure, purpose, and harmony in themselves. While perception and feeling are raised to the universality of the spirit, thought not only renounces its

hostility against nature but enjoys itself in nature. Feeling, joy, and pleasure are sanctioned and justified so that nature and freedom, sensuousness and reason, find in their unity their right and their gratification.[13]

Marcuse omits Nietzsche from his list of exponents of aesthetic consciousness (perhaps an oversight), but he does evoke him as the harbinger

of a new reality principle [which] breaks the repressive context and anticipates the liberation from the archaic heritage. . . . For Nietzsche, the liberation depends on the reversal of the sense of guilt; mankind must come to associate the bad conscience not with affirmation but with the denial of the life instincts, not with the rebellion but with the acceptance of the repressive ideals.[14]

To speak of the solution as aesthetic does not tell us how the unrepressed self will be created. Leaving aside the pragmatic question, a number of other questions arise. How accurate are Marcuse and Schiller in representing the aesthetic? What of the disciplinary and repressive side of aesthetic consciousness that we find in Aschenbach's career, for example? And how desirable is such a solution? The fully realized artist (Marcuse is envisaging a society of artists) is an aristocratic character, whose triumphant emergence in the world would coercively eliminate ordinary men and ordinary life. Rilke's Nietzschean formulation is memorable:

Not for all time will the artist live side by side with ordinary men. As soon as the artist—the more flexible and deeper type among them—becomes rich and virile, as soon as he *lives* what now he merely *dreams*, man will degenerate and gradually die out. The artist is eternity protruding into time.[15]

Despite Marcuse's vision of a utopia of play, his view of nonrepressive civilization is remote from anarchy. Unlike Leo Bersani, a romantic anarchist who conceives of desire as fragmentary, scattered, disordered, the very antithesis of reason, Marcuse imagines desire as a simulacrum for the reason it renounces. "Civilization begins when the primary objective—namely, integral satisfaction of needs—is effectively renounced."[16] In imagining an *integral* satisfaction as an alternative to repressive civilization, Marcuse is doing little more than appropriating the totalizing habit of Hegelian thought, producing, so to speak, a rationalism of desire that has the features of its adversary. And even if the Marcusan solution were attractive, the question of its possible realization would arise. Marcuse has no conception of how individual desire becomes collective desire without coercive imposition, which would, of course, contradict the very meaning of desire by eliminating individual freedom. Indeed, it could be argued that desire is by its very nature individual and that collective desire is an oxymoron, which would immediately abort the utopian project.

The extraordinary affinities between Marcuse and Norman O. Brown, whose book *Life Against Death* (1959) appeared only four years after *Eros and Civilization*, confirm the operation of the zeitgeist, the sense that a new psychological tyranny had been created by the very discipline that stood for psychological liberation and that any new liberation would have to occur within the categories of the discipline, that is, by valuing the repressed terms in the Freudian dualisms. The gesture is a familiar one. Reformations are not created ex nihilo; they receive their authority from an interpretation of the very texts on which the established authority bases itself.

Like Marcuse, Brown radicalizes Freud's insights. Whereas Freud speaks of all human beings as more or less neurotic or as more or less diseased, Brown characterizes man in Nietzschean fashion as himself a disease. And the disease is to be found in the repression of the true "essence" of man, desire: ". . . the essence of man consists not, as Descartes maintained, in thinking, but in desiring."[17] To speak of desire as an essence, as Brown does, is self-contradictory since essence belongs to an antithetic rationalist discourse. The radicalizing of insight and language is so strong that a slippage occurs, for instance, in the chapter "Neuroses and History" from neuroses to madness. According to Brown the so-called normal (neurotic) condition of man is insane. Modern literature has provided graphic instances of this condition in the characters of the underground man in Dostoevsky's *Notes from Underground* and of Kurtz in Conrad's *Heart of Darkness*, among others. Kurtz may be the most compelling instance, for his madness is perceived as a direct result of his having raised reason, his own reason, to the position of divinity. In carrying on the Nietzschean legacy, Brown anticipates the post-structuralist attack on man, on a humanism that has to be surpassed.

Like Marcuse, he turns to art as an anti-repressive force that encourages polymorphous perversity and regression to infantile eroticism. As in the case with Marcuse, one may wonder about the accuracy or adequacy of Brown's representation of art, which stresses (one might say overstresses) its childlike aspect at the expense of the philosophic mind, and affirms Dionysus at the expense of Apollo with a rather vague concession that the murderous risks of the Dionysian must be obviated by a reconstruction of the Dionysian ego.

> The work of contructing a Dionysian ego is immense, but there are signs that it is already underway. If we can discern the Dionysian witches' brew in the upheavals of modern history— in the sexology of de Sade and the politics of Hitler—we can also discern in the romantic reaction the entry of Dionysus into consciousness. . . . The only alternative to the witches' brew is psychoanalytical consciousness, which is not the Apollonian scholasticism of orthodox psychoanalysis, but consciousness embracing and affirming instinctual reality—Dionysian consciousness.[18]

The distinctive feature of Brown's argument is his affinity for mystical and religious thought. Here, as we might expect, he is sharply critical of Freud's hostility toward religion. Freud viewed religion, as he viewed art, as institutional neurosis, not as an instrument of liberation. Though critical of what he understands as D. H. Lawrence's puritan attitude toward sexuality in insisting, as Lawrence does, on the spiritual conditions of sexuality (he calls him "a paradoxically conservative philosopher of sexuality"),[19] Brown shares with Lawrence an appreciation of religious intuitions of the sensual mysteries. The final chapter of *Life Against Death* is titled "The Resurrection of the Body," imagined under the auspices of Dionysus rather than Christ.[20]

There is something of a contradiction in Brown's view of religion. On the one hand, Brown praises both religion and psychoanalysis for acknowledging and respecting the hiddenness of the divine presence and psychic reality, respectively.[21] Brown quotes Pascal: "all appearance indicates neither a total exclusion nor a manifest presence of divinity, but the presence of a God who hides himself. . . . God being thus hidden, every religion which does not affirm that God is hidden, is not true; and every religion which does not give the reason of it is not instructive." Brown remarks: "Psychoanalysis passes the test." But in a passage that precedes the one I have just cited, Brown celebrates Christ's doing away "with the veil" that Jewish law has imposed on spiritual reality.[22] It is as if Brown wanted a synthesis which would resolve the contradiction between mystification and demystification.

Since both Marcuse and Brown claim to be working within the Freudian dispensation, it is fair to judge the fidelity or infidelity of their rendering of Freud's thought. The effect of Marcuse's and Brown's performances is illicitly to dialecticize Freud (in the Hegelian manner) by introducing a third synthetic term, where there is none in Freud. Nowhere in Freud's work is the dualistic character of his thought more in evidence than in the late great essays *Beyond the Pleasure Principle*, *The Ego and the Id* and *Civilization and Its Discontents*. The essays represent a process in which Freud tries to discover the most comprehensive and the most precise terms to represent the struggle. If the process is unresolved, what remains persistent in the Freudian speculation is the field of dualities that cannot be resolved or transcended. "Our views have from the very first been *dualistic*, and today they are even more definitely dualistic than before—now that we describe the opposition as being, not between ego-instincts but between life instincts and death instincts."[23]

Here are some of the dualities: consciousness vs. unconsciousness, coherent ego vs. repressed, ego instincts vs. sexual, aggressive instincts vs. erotic, death instincts vs. life. The argument in *Beyond the Pleasure Principle* moves rapidly from one set of terms to another in a manner that is often tortuous and unclear. It moves by fits and starts, goes off in a particular direction only to hesitate because it lacks evidence. If there is a resolution to the succession of conflicts, the resolution is death—that is an inanimate state, which produces "the pleasure" common to all the drives—the pleasure of a complete extinction of suffering.

> . . . it is tempting to pursue to its logical conclusion the hypothesis that all instincts tend towards the restoration of an earlier state of things.[24]

> . . . If we firmly maintain the exclusively conservative nature of

instincts, we cannot arrive at any other notions as to the origin and aim of life. . . . What we are left with is the fact that the organism wishes to die only in its own fashion.[25]

In *Civilization and Its Discontents*, Freud extends his dualism to the relationship between self and civilization. Civilization itself is irreducibly ambiguous in its relation to the self. It is at once a condition of selfhood and a source of suffering. It is the product of a necessary repression (a defense against the destructive consequences of an uninhibited pursuit of the pleasure principle) and the cause of repression.

The ambiguous role of civilization in the fate of the self provokes an ambivalent attitude in Freud. He is a critic of its excesses in inducing pain.

> I have endeavored to guard myself against the enthusiastic prejudice which holds that our civilization is the most precious thing that we possess or could acquire and that its path will necessarily lead to benefits of unimagined perfection. [An Enlightenment prejudice, one might add.] I can at least listen without indignation to the critic who is of the opinion that when one surveys the aims of cultural endeavor and the means it employs, one is bound to come to the conclusion that the whole effort is not worth the trouble, and that the outcome of it can only be a state of affairs which the individual will be unable to tolerate.[26]

If civilization is supposed to contain the aggressive impulses, its severities often exacerbate them, provoking a return of the repressed. Freud advocates a mitigation of the severities of civilization and its superegoistic agencies in the psychic life of the individual. At the same time, he is clearly committed to "civilized" values. Writing in the aftermath of World War I, he speaks of the absolute necessity of controlling the aggressive impulses, and in his moving conclusion to *Civilization and Its Discontents*, he expresses the hope that "Eros will make an effort to assert itself in the struggle with his equally immortal adversary," Thanatos.[27] Note, however, the Manichean language. Freud envisages no permanent victory for Eros. The forces of Thanatos, of aggression, are eternally embedded in human life. If the human condition is inescapably ambiguous and dualistic, Freud's attitude is correspondingly ambivalent.

In acknowledging the *repressive* character of civilization, Freud condemns neither repression nor civilization: he understands the necessity for both. He possesses no third term, no alternative to the dualities of consciousness vs. unconsciousness, ego instinct vs. sexual instinct. For Freud, the totalizing syntheses of German thought are fictions of the repressive project of civilization. Freud's dualism permits him to respond to the competing claims of pleasure and reality, of sensuality and asceticism, to appreciate the continually shifting balances of psychic energies in the life of civilization. As with Mann in *Death in Venice*, the ambivalent view is empowering. The ego may aim at unity and coherence, but it is not coterminous with the self: it is only a component of the self. Nor is it given a securely controlling position in the hierarchy of the elements that compose the self—as, for example, reason holds in the rationalist hierarchy.

The argument for illimitable desire effectively obliterates the distinction between reason and desire on the analogy of a revolutionary dialectic in which the repressed term overthrows the repressive term, absorbs and transforms it in a new synthesis. Desire has become the representative of liberty and democracy. It asserts the right of everyone in the polis to satisfaction and fulfillment. In contrast, reason tends to be authoritative, controlling, directive. Reason has had a long association with universal democracy since the Enlightenment. But its democratic aspect may be seen as a temporary effect of its own revolutionary role in overthrowing supernatural authority: God and his worldly ecclesiastical instruments. By arrogating to itself the idea of Man, reason masked for a time its own hegemonic conception of life in which it prevailed over desire. The new synthesis under the aegis of desire may nevertheless prove to be a mystification of a new despotism of the hitherto repressed term.

Both Marcuse and Brown wrote in the fifties before the social explosions of the sixties, well before the 1968 international student revolt occurs, in which erotic and passional liberation is at the top of the revolutionary agenda. The locus of revolutionary activity becomes the university rather than the factory, its agents students rather than workers and its grievances, psychic and moral rather than economic and moral. In France, Gilles Deleuze and Felix Guattari's *Anti-Oedipus* (1972) provides a theoretical representa tion of the revolutionary explosion. The idiom of the book is a potpourri of Marx, Freud, Saussurian linguistics, and structuralism. The book is part analysis and part manifesto, at once brilliant and exasperating. The enemy is capitalism in its familial form, the oedipal structure seen as the chief nexus of repression.

Deleuze and Guattari in their prose give us the energy of what they call the desiring machine beyond anything conveyed in the writing of Marcuse or Brown.

> It is at work everywhere, functioning smoothly at times, at other times in fits and starts. It breathes, it heats, it eats. It shits and fucks. What a mistake to have ever said *the* id. Everywhere *it* is machines—real ones, not figurative ones: machines driving other machines, machines being driven by other machines, with all the necessary couplings and connections. An organ-machine is plugged into an energy-source-machine: the one produces a flow that the other interrupts. The breast is a machine that produces milk, and the mouth a machine coupled to it. The mouth of the anorexic wavers between several functions: its possessor is uncertain as to whether it is an eating-machine, an anal machine, a talking-machine, or a breathing-machine (asthma attacks). Hence we are all handymen: each with his little machines. For every organ-machine, an energy-machine: all the time, flows and interruptions. Judge Schreber has sunbeams in his ass. *A solar anus.* And rest assured that it works: Judge Schreber feels something, produces something, and is capable of explaining the process theoretically. Something is produced: the effects of a machine, not mere metaphors.[28]

Their modernity or postmodernity shows in their commitment to the machine (they have no use for the organic). What they value is the boundlessness of desire to which all codes are inimical. In effect, they revalue desire, converting it from a negative, with its connotations of want and lack, to a positive, conveying sheer unprocessed energy or life. What negates desire is, in their view, its insertion in the order of representation. Discourse, representation, and codes are modalities of repression that betray "the savage flows of desire." Deleuze and Guattari fail to explain how their own representation of desire exempts itself from the category of repression.

There is an irony in the fact that Michel Foucault wrote a

preface to *Anti-Oedipus*, for if the work of Deleuze and Guattari represents a culminating expression of the revolution of desire, Foucault's three-volume *History of Sexuality*, composed a decade later, represents the most powerful "reaction" that we have against it. But before I turn to Foucault, I want to look briefly at one of the most significant and intelligent responses to the intellectual and imaginative ethos of l968, Lionel Trilling's *Sincerity and Authenticity*, originally the Charles Eliot Norton lectures at Harvard University in 1969–70. The lectures were delivered at the very moment when student uprisings were taking place there. Though Trilling does not explicitly refer to the events of the year, they are sufficiently present in the work of writers whom Trilling addresses: Sartre, Marcuse, Brown, and R. D. Laing.

In the final chapter, "The Authentic Unconscious," Trilling begins somewhat deviously with a question about the loss of authority that narrative has suffered in the contemporary period. His real object is to account for psychoanalysis' recent failure to gain credence. According to Trilling, the failure lies in the fact that psychoanalysis depends upon narrative, and narrative has come to be seen as a fictional construction that betrays the authenticity of unconscious life. Trilling's exposition of the connection between psychoanalysis and narrative is cryptic and unsatisfying, but it does serve to introduce the theme of authenticity, which Trilling sees as the basis for the new revolutionary consciousness. Sartre is the crucial figure, having provided in the second chapter of *Being and Nothingness* a very powerful formulation of the theme, a curious one, since he opposes authenticity to the unconscious or at least to the psychoanalytic unconscious.

Sartre's objection to the psychoanalytic unconscious is twofold: ontological and moral. Sartre doubts its existence, because the id (Freud's version of the unconscious) can be known only by hypothesis; it cannot be directly observed. Morally, Sartre objects to Freud's division of the psychic whole into two, a condition that contributes to what Sartre considers the gravest of modern sins, bad faith. The division of the psyche enables the ego to displace responsibility to the id. Since the ego cannot control the id, it cannot be charged with responsibility for behavior which proceeds from the unconscious. Trilling quotes Sartre: "I *am* the ego, but I *am not* the id, which is to say, 'I am my own psychic phenomena insofar as I establish them in their conscious reality.' "[29] Sartre believes in the theoretical possibility of a coherent, unitary self in which appearance and reality authentically coincide, though psychic division seems the condition of actual life. Trilling defends psychoanalysis against the charge of bad faith by pointing to its effort to overcome the dualism: "Wherever id was, there ego should be"; the ego must learn to assume responsibility for the id.

But Sartre's picture of the psychoanalytic self as a duality or as a series of dualities remains essentially accurate. His rejection of the duality from the side of consciousness reverses the Marcusan or Brownian rejection from the side of unconsciousness. The desire for unified consciousness notwithstanding, psychoanalytic "authenticity" entails an irreducible duality of being.

The split subject means perpetual struggle—it means, among other things, that the self must negotiate a dual loyalty to itself and to civilization. Trilling's commitment to the psychoanalytic split subject is the basis of his critique of the bad faith of so-called authentic being (whether under the sign of consciousness or of unconsciousness), which rejects the claims of civilization or society. For what is the consequence of standing completely outside of civilization (assuming that such a stance is possible) but madness?

> Yet the doctrine that madness is health, that madness is liberation and authenticity, receives a happy welcome from a consequential part of the educated public. And when we have given due weight to the likelihood that those who respond positively to the doctrine don't have it in mind to go mad, let alone insane—it is characteristic of the intellectual life of our culture that it fosters a form of assent which does not involve actual credence—we must yet take it to be significant of our circumstance that many among us find it gratifying to entertain the thought that alienation is to be overcome only by the completeness of alienation, and that alienation completed is not a deprivation or deficiency but a potency.[30]

(We may glimpse in this ironic formulation Lawrence's doctrine of self-responsibility.) Trilling speaks of such an advocacy as cant, and he satirizes its claim to authenticity by inviting us to imagine what true and false means in this discourse. "The falsities of an alienated social reality are rejected in favor of an upward psychopathic mobility to the point of divinity. . . ."[31]

Indeed, the argument for authentic unified being produces its own divisions and contradictions. Trilling, for instance, acutely notes that Marcuse is not willing to give up on the idea of character, which depends on the traditional role of the family. Marcuse is distressed by "the devolution of the power of the superego," the result of the diminished authority of the family, which in turn results in a failure in individual development. Trilling wryly wonders whether "some Hegelian device will properly resolve the contradiction between Marcuse's predilection for the strongly defined character-structure that necessity entails and his polemical commitment to a Utopia which will do away with necessity." [32]

One of the implicit objects of Trilling's critique is an early work of Foucault, *Madness and Civilization*. David Cooper, R. D. Laing's collaborator, cites with approval Foucault's characterization of madness as "the [true] voicing of the realization that I am (or you are) Christ." [33] So it comes as something of a surprise to discover that in his last work, *The History of Sexuality*, Foucault offers us a critique of the revolution of desire from within, the product of a man who has lived and suffered the "liberation."

The History of Sexuality is the most original post-Freudian discussion of sexual desire we have. According to Foucault, the triumph of sexual desire had occurred long ago, and the evidence for it can be found in the discourses that testify to its putative repression. He rejects the hypothesis of repression that has dominated our understanding of modern sexuality and which in his view constitutes an event rather than an explanation of the history of sexuality. The truth of our sexual experience, Foucault argues, lies not in its repression but in its expression: that is to say, in the extraordinary variety of discourse about sex since the sixteenth and seventeenth centuries. Analytical discourse "yield[s] multiple effects of displacement, intensification, reorientation and modification of desire itself." [34] In other words, the discourse is ars erotica, multiplying new desires and new pleasures. In Foucault's conception, the displacements of discourse are not signs of repression, but stimulations of desire. What we are, do, feel, desire is not represented or repressed by language, but is in a sense created by it.

For Foucault all the agencies for regulating sexual activity are agencies of sexual expressiveness. He doesn't so much dismiss the fact of repression as change its meaning. He sees it as a major tactic in a pleasure-power game for sexual incitement. Foucault expresses in a strikingly unfamiliar way what may be the evident truth of erotic desire, that it is intensified under "repression." Foucault's "history" is a series of dense, cryptic suggestions about changes that in his view have taken place in the deployment of sexuality through the centuries—for instance, the change that took place between the deployment of sexuality by the church through the confession in which virtue and sin are the operative categories and the medicalization of sexuality in which the sinful becomes the perverse and the pathological. In naming a sin, in compelling it to be confessed, in analyzing it, the energies of the sin (or the illness) are brought to light, developed, expanded, multiplied. In a sense, both the church and medicine invent the sins and diseases that they condemn. And those sins and diseases survive the condemnation. They are, as it were, secularized into the natural experiences of mankind.

Foucault's critique of this history is as surprising as the history itself. Having challenged the repressive hypothesis on epistemological grounds, he goes on to see it as a concealment of the tyranny of sexuality in our lives. Indeed, all power tends to gravitate toward sexuality. We have come to feel that sex alone gives intelligibility to the self, that it is the "hidden aspect and generative principle of meaning."[35] It is ironic that we self-delusively think of this tyranny as liberation. Foucault's reaction against the tyranny of sexuality can be read as movement toward asceticism or as a utopian conception of "a different economy of bodies and pleasures" in which sex has its place, but is no longer the essence, the "hidden" principle of man. Foucault has in effect elicited the essentialist character of the sexual revolution.[36]

Is Freud the proto-liberationist, the father of the sexual revolution that Foucault makes him out to be? In rejecting the view that the sexual factor is the sole determinant in human life, Freud explained why psychoanalysis was obliged to concentrate on the sexual factor.

> Psychoanalysis has never forgotten that there are instinctual forces as well which are not sexual. It was based on a sharp distinction between the sexual instincts and the ego-instincts, and, in spite of all objections, it has maintained not that the

neuroses are derived from sexuality but that their origin is due to a conflict between the ego and sexuality. Nor has it any conceivable reason for disputing the existence or significance of the ego-instincts while it pursues the part played by the sexual instincts in illness and in ordinary life. It has simply been its fate to begin by concerning itself with the sexual instincts because the transference neuroses made them the most easily accessible to examination and because it was incumbent on it to study what other people had neglected.[37]

One effect of focusing on the sexual factor is to invite the charge of reductionism against Freud. He has demystified our experience, substituting for its presumed variety, a singular hidden reality, the sexual motive. Moreover, the current vogue of perspectivism becomes a justification for viewing Freud's claim for the centrality of the sexual factor as a repression of the full range of perspectives from which we may understand human reality.

Freud was a target of such criticism in his own lifetime, and he understood it as a conservative, even reactionary obstacle to intellectual discovery, when prematurely made against a newly evolving body of thought. In his essay "A History of the Psychoanalytic Movement" Freud criticizes the role "played by the relativity of all knowledge, and the right of the personality to put an artificial construction on the data of knowledge according to individual taste" as inimical to scientific advance.[38] It denies what science requires, the possibility of objective truth. The deviations of Adler and Jung, whatever truth they may contain, represent for Freud an obscuring of the sexual motive at the moment when its reality was being established in the face of hostility by the general culture. At the same time Freud in the scientific spirit does not claim special privileges for his theory. "None of us can guess what the ultimate judgment of mankind about our theoretical efforts will be."[39] I understand this humility about his own efforts as an endorsement of the possibility of other, even contrary perspectives, but with the understanding that at any given period in history a particular perspective gains authority and is allowed to develop a body of knowledge unimpeded by the clamor of talk about the relativity of all knowledge. Without the privileging of a perspective, scientific progress is impossible. In any event, in concentrating on "the sexual etiology of neuroses" and on the sexual factor in the total life of the individual and civilization, Freud did not see himself as the precursor of what we understand today as sexual liberation, that is, of the version that Foucault characterizes as tyranny.

It is illuminating in this connection to compare Freud's emphasis on the sexual factor with Marx's stress on the economic. If the essential man for Marx is *homo economicus,* it is not in the sense that man is an ethical or rational being for Plato or Aristotle. Economics is not the telos of human development for Marx. On the contrary, his revolutionary program in a sense entails the transcendence of the economic in the mastery of the laws of economic development. It would of course be foolish to claim that Freud analogously advocates the transcendence of the sexual. Genital sexual maturity is a value in psychoanalytic thought. Freud fully understood the price people pay for a repressive sexual morality. In "'Civilized' Sexual Morality and Modern Nervous Illness," he writes:

> It is one of the obvious social injustices that the standard of civilization should demand from everyone the same conduct of sexual life—conduct which can be followed without any difficulty by some people, thanks to their organization, but which imposes the heaviest psychical sacrifices on others; though, indeed, the injustice is as a rule wiped out by disobedience to the injustices of morality.[40]

This is a view that I construe as humane without being liberationist in the contemporary sense. The passing of moral judgments on sexual behavior or its repression is inescapable. But the making of such judgments does not reflect on Freud's essential achievement. In order to liberate sexuality as a subject matter for study, Freud had to purge it of moral connotations. It impoverishes the Freudian text to read Freud as either advocate or antagonist of sexuality and its expressions. He is a student of its complexity. The goal of Freudian theory and practice is a self-knowlege that implicates our sexuality beyond the moralizing language of virtue and vice.

What then are the ethical implications of Freud's theory? Since Freud's investigations concern the contents of the psyche, which consists of dreams, thoughts and volitions, the sexual factor cannot remain morally neutral: it involves what in other discourses are moral and spiritual questions. One can see this at once in comparing physical illness with psychic illness. In becoming physically ill, one's human dignity need not be affected, whereas the loss of one's mind, the failure to master one's sexuality, for example, threatens one's moral integrity.

We might approach the question of the meaning of sexuality in Freud's conception, its moral status, so to speak, by comparing it with the pornographic imagination. We have a precedent for this in the work of Steven Marcus. In *The Other Victorians*, Marcus characterizes pornography as a reaction against the repression of sexuality in the Victorian period. In an audacious exercise in "utopian" construction, he imagines a pornotopia, a counter-image to Victorian society, in which all of life is sexualized. In a pornotopia, pornography would, so to speak, come out of the closet and in a sense cease to be pornography, which gives pleasure in its antithetic furtiveness and secrecy. According to Marcus, the effect of such a realization would be the dissolution of personality and character and the emptying of sex or sexuality of meaning. If high Victorianism represses sex, pornography or rather a pornotopia would render it meaningless.

Psychoanalysis is an alternative to Victorianism on the one hand and to pornography on the other. Marcus values psychoanalysis for creating an intellectual distance from sexual beliefs that permits discussion of sex in "a neutral way," and goes on to claim for psychoanalysis the distinction of having for the first time conferred upon human sexuality "a meaning, using the word 'meaning' in the sense put to it by philosophy."[41] By neutrality, Marcus undoubtedly means a view of the subject without moral prejudices. The scientist neither affirms nor denies. He tries to understand and to explain. Philosophical "meaning," however, has a resonance that takes us beyond sheer objectivity: it suggests significance, value, even belief. Meaning, Marcus reminds us, depends upon distinctions and discriminations in which something means or signifies at the expense of other things that do not. Pornography, on the other hand, obliterates distinction in its complete sexualization of life. For Freud, sex is not the telos of human life: he never proposed the view that human liberation consisted in the removal of all obstacles to sexual satisfaction. On the contrary, he appears to condemn this view in the following passage from his essay, "On

the Universal Tendency to Debasement in the Sphere of Love"
(1912):

> In times in which there were no difficulties standing in the way
> of sexual satisfaction, such as perhaps during the decline of the
> ancient civilizations, love became worthless and life empty, and
> strong reaction-formations were required to restore indispens-
> able affective values. In this connection it may be claimed that
> the ascetic current in Christianity created psychical values for
> love which pagan antiquity was never able to confer on it. This
> current assumed its greatest importance with the ascetic monks,
> whose lives were almost entirely occupied with the struggle against
> libidinal temptation.[42]

This passage gives us an interesting clue in the word "obstacles." Obstacles produce the displacements and sublimations that
characterize both the sexual and nonsexual behavior of human
beings. What is of utmost importance and interest in Freud's work
is not the centrality of the sexual motive, (i.e., sexual determinism), but rather its capacity for displacement which enables Freud
to exercize his interpretive genius in tracking the activities not only
of Dora and the Rat Man, but of Michelangelo and Leonardo da
Vinci as well. His achievement consists not in the repetitious discovery of the sexual motive in human activity but rather in its
countless and various sublimations in the cultural life. And here
we have the answer to the charge that Freud is a reductionist or a
sexual determinist or an essentializer of sexual experience. The
power of psychoanalysis consists precisely in its capacity to give
narrative accounts (not the only possible accounts, to be sure) of
the variety and complexity of human experience.

Freud's characterization of the storyteller in his famous essay
"On the Uncanny" applies to his own narrative powers:

> The story-teller has a peculiarly directive influence over us;
> by means of the states of mind into which he can put us and the
> expectations he can rouse in us, he is able to guide the current of
> our emotions, dam it up in one direction and make it flow in
> another, and *he often obtains a great variety of effects from the
> same material* [emphasis added].[43]

His view of Michelangelo's Moses is the opposite of reductive (to
offer one example): it reflects his belief in the power of the ethical

will to transform passion—in this case the aggressive passion. Freud reads the sculpture as an allegory of Michelangelo's own passionate nature.

> The Moses of legend and tradition had a hasty temper and was subject to fits of *passion*. It was in a transport of divine wrath of this kind that he slew an Egyptian who was maltreating an Israelite, and had to flee out of the land into the wilderness; and it was in a similar passion that he broke the Tables of the Law, inscribed by God Himself. Tradition, in recording such a characteristic, is unbiased, and preserves the impression of a great personality who once lived. But Michelangelo has placed a different Moses on the tomb of the Pope, one superior to the historical or traditional Moses. He has modified the theme of the broken Tables; he does not let Moses break them in his wrath, but makes him be influenced by the danger that they will be broken and calm that wrath, or at any rate prevent it from becoming an act. In this way he has added something new and more than human to the figure of Moses, so that the giant frame with its tremendous physical power becomes only a concrete expression of the highest mental achievement that is possible in a man, that of struggling successfully against an inward passion for the sake of a cause to which he has devoted himself.[44]

The sculpture becomes "a warning to [Michelangelo] himself, thus [enabling him to rise] in self-criticism, superior to his own nature."[45] And we may read the essay as an expression of Freud's own effort to achieve self-mastery. My example of a passion requiring mastery is of an aggressive passion. Freud understood as well the potential violence in uninhibited sexual desire (a violence to oneself as to others) and he knew that the pleasure principle was in a sense served by its antithesis the reality principle. Freud was interested in the drama of displacement and substitution, which deflects desire from its destructive course—to be sure, at the price of suffering. (I might note here that contemporary hermeneutic practice has only recently begun to find in Freud's interpretive practice inspiration for nonreductionist readings of texts.)

Freud was more interested in sexuality than he was in sex, and by that I mean thinking about sex rather than the physical act itself. Indeed, sexuality and thinking were, in Freud's view, companions. Freud himself stated the case with characteristic incisiveness when he deplored the repression of sexual thought and feeling in women.

> [Women's] upbringing forbids their concerning themselves intellectually with sexual problems though they nevertheless feel extremely curious about them, and frightens them by condemning such curiosity as unwomanly and a sign of a sinful disposition. In this way, they are scared away from *any* form of thinking, and knowledge loses its value for them. The prohibition of thought extends beyond the sexual field, partly through unavoidable association, partly automatically, like the prohibition of thought about religion among men, or the prohibition of thought about loyalty among faithful subjects.[46]

The transgressive character of sexuality becomes a metaphor for intellectual adventure.

The history of culture can be conceived of as a succession of the "privileging" of one or another prohibition. In the time of Plato and Socrates the most significant prohibition may have been of a religious kind, which provoked the transgressive originality of Socrates' thought. The same could be said of Galileo and Copernicus. For Freud, the sexual prohibition had acquired a force that became an implicit challenge to revolutionary thought. A prohibition is not the same as repression, which is deep and unconscious and triumphs by causing one to forget what is repressed. A prohibition is a provocation, an invitation to transgress in action and in thought. Sexuality for Freud was the treacherous area of darkness that needed to be explored and illuminated by the light of reason and that demanded the most powerful and most courageous of intellects. I think Foucault in his critique of the hypothesis of repression underestimates (from the perspective of our current liberationist ethos) the counterforce of the prohibitive sexual ideology of Victorian culture and in particular of Viennese society.

What was true for Freud may no longer be true for contemporary thinkers. In answer to the question, "do you think that understanding sexuality is central for understanding who we are?" Foucault answered that he found sex (doubtless meaning speculation about it) "boring."[47] The reason, one might surmise, is that with sexual "liberation," the prohibitions have vanished and every entry into the field of sexual experience is, so to speak, through an open door. What was an adventure has become an exercise in repetition.

Sexual problems persist and they are the concern of therapy and medicine. There are moral and philosophical discourses that have assimilated sexuality to the ethical life. But the particular challenge to thought that sexuality offered to Freud has disappeared, or if it has not disappeared, has been transformed. Questions of sexual identity, of the relations between sex and gender have become the new locus of intellectual explorations. Foucault's testimony of boredom (the discipline of the self became his main interest) may perhaps be unjust to the speculative possibilities offered by these new questions. And yet one does not experience in the new speculations, the transgressive force of the earlier explorations by Freud. Having triumphed, sexual discourse encounters little or no resistance. There is no longer anything to transgress. Hundreds of theories present themselves to an audience supersaturated with theoretical and practical sexual discourse. Freudian thought may have become a victim of its own success.

How does this view of psychoanalysis square with Foucault's view that the hypothesis of repression does not so much describe psychic reality as it does an event, the culminating event, in the so-called liberation of sexuality in the modern period, so-called because it has in effect become a new tyranny? My reading of Freud clearly resists Foucault's view. If we consider the dualistic character of Freud's thought in terms of the rival claims of the pleasure principle and the reality principle, we must conclude that Foucault's Freud is a reinvention or sign for a particular Freudian legacy, for which Freud cannot be held responsible.

A generation ago a contest took place for the legacy between the orthodox Freudians who had overvalued the reality principle and the proto-liberationists Herbert Marcuse and Norman O. Brown, who wished to resolve the Freudian dualism (illicitly, I believe) to the pleasure principle. That battle had the aspect of a scholastic quarrel, with each side arguing from authority: that is, from its understanding of Freud. It resembled the schismatic fights between, let us say, Trotskyists and Stalinists over the Marxist inheritance. The liberationists clearly won the day in the cultural life. It seems to me Foucault is right in his diagnosis of our cultural situation, but he is misleading in his characterization of Freud's intended contribution to it.

More than a description of a psychological and cultural condition, the hypothesis of repression has become a powerful polemic against repression and for desire. If it has not directly caused changes in family and social structures, the repressive hypothesis and the larger discourse of desire of which it is part have paralleled those changes.

Evidence of these changes can be found in the work of Heinz Kohut. According to Steven Marcus' informed and lucid account, Kohut and his associates discovered that "the classical neurotic patient as first observed by Freud seemed to be gradually disappearing and was being steadily replaced by people who suffered from various kinds of what is known as ego-syntonic character pathology. In particular, as time passed, it began to be evident that a series of narcissistic disorders were presenting themselves as the emerging prototypical personality formation of the current era of our culture."[48] The contemporary neurotic experiences feelings of emptiness or feelings of fragmentation and discontinuity. His or her narcissism is based, then, on a lack of "self-esteem." Kohut attributes the new neurotic type to the weakening of the Oedipal structure, that is, to the dissolution of family constraints, which manifest themselves in parental "commands, prohibitions, praise, scolding and punishment" and contribute to the development of the ego. "Children in the past were '*over*stimulated' by the 'threateningly close . . . emotional . . . life of their parents' "; now they are *under*stimulated by parents whom they experience as "threateningly distant."[49] The absence of constraint and direction in the family life is reproduced in the wider social life in which permissiveness rather than restriction characterizes the prevailing ethos.

I would like to suggest a connection between Foucault's view of the history of sexuality and Kohut's discovery of a new neurotic type in contemporary society. The sense of emptiness and fragmentation Kohut describes and that one finds in contemporary fiction—for instance, in the work of so-called minimalist writers Donald Barthelme, Ann Beattie, and Raymond Carver—is connected with the discourse of uncensored desire. It can be understood as the result of what happens when desires are unbound, free to "imagine" their course irrespective of obstacles and resistances. They exhaust themselves, lose their energy and terminate in the experience of nullity. Beattie's minimalist fiction is a particularly striking representative case in its bleak tone and the absence of a coherent will. The high hopes, the exhilarations of the 1960s have produced a kind of "hangover." She gives us in her first novel, *Chilly Scenes of Winter* (1976) an artful style of desultoriness. The life of a character in Ann Beattie's fiction is represented through uneventful external details.

> Charles goes back to bed. He sees that Sam is already in bed in his room. He pulls the covers up over himself and falls asleep. He wakes up at five o'clock when the alarm goes off. He gets up, pushes in the button, and goes back to bed. . . .[50]

Nothing happens, but the very fact that Beattie tells her story in the mode of realistic narrative in which events follow one another in a logical consecutive manner preserves a sense of expectation and even promise: something might happen. But it never does.

In associating Foucault with Kohut I am in effect altering Foucault's argument—or at least suggesting an extension of the one that he seems to intend. Where Foucault speaks of the tyranny of sexual desire, Kohut implies its enervation. Is this a contradiction? I think not. It is precisely the elevation of sexual desire, indeed of desire as a supreme value, that entails as one of its consequences its enervation. What keeps desire alive is the sense of resistance, of the play of other values, energies, faculties. Illimitable desire generates impossible and self-defeating expectations which produce the experience of despair.

One need not share Foucault's assumptions about discourse to appreciate his powerful insight into the tyranny of desire, which does not depend upon those assumptions. Bersani's protest that desire in its fragmentary, discontinuous condition, its "natural" condition, has been and continues to be repressed masks the cultural fact that the revolution of desire has in fact succeeded.

Does this mean that the reconstruction of the Dionysian ego that Brown advocated has indeed taken place? That life has been made over by the sensuousness of art? Or that "surplus repression" is a thing of the past? The "revolution" has not been successful on its own terms. Like all revolutionary triumphs, this one is not what its proponents meant at all. It has been first a triumph of discourse, as Foucault has demonstrated. Such a triumph enables new attitudes, permits new feelings, creates new expectations, new power concentrations. But the "success" has revealed the vacuity of liberationist talk about desire. The refusal or incapacity of the revolutionaries of desire to acknowledge their "victory" is their refusal or incapacity to acknowledge its bitter fruits. The idea of illimitable desire has infected the various institutions of social life: family, school, workplace, and the marketplace, and as with every new "successful" revolution, the revolution of desire has produced its discontents.

7 ɛ» The Freudian Narrative and The Case of Jacques Lacan

Foucault's reading of Freud, whatever view we may take of it, is an appropriation of psychoanalysis on a terrain Freud did not define. Jacques Lacan's distinction, or his claim to it, is that he is the truest of Freudians, in a sense more faithful to the original inspiration than the master himself, and he can be thought of as Freud's coeval. According to Lacan, the locus of "meaning" in Freud is the unconscious, which for Lacan is virtually synonymous with desire. Lacan's prose—difficult, even preposterous—is an attempt, unique in the annals of psychoanalytic thought, to render the movement of desire itself.

Lacan's true (not orthodox) Freudian stance puts him in even-handed opposition, on the one hand, to the ego psychologists who "depict . . . the ego as an agent of adaptibility, synthesis and integration—an agency of the total person—thereby giving ever greater sway to the consciousness in determining being"[1] and, on the other hand, to radical revisionists like Deleuze and Guattari, who believe "that one can recover presocial desiring individualism, circumvent the triadic Holy family and ally Desire to the collectivity rather than to a power hierarchy."[2] Lacan condemns both the repressive privileging of the ego and the deluded, because impossible, utopianism of desire.

If this were all to be said about Lacan, he would be little more than an epigone of Freud, although an important one, given the uniqueness of his voice on the contemporary scene. In fact, the balance or tension in Lacan's thought clearly favors the cause of desire. Lacan's lucidity about the impossible project of desire does not prevent him from declaring that "interpretation is directed toward desire. Desire, in fact, is interpretation itself."[3]

The Lacanian affinity for desire is a predilection for truth, for the real, not for its impossible, indeed undesirable, satisfactions. If desire is the reality or truth of the self and its satisfaction is an impossibility, the human condition must be inescapably tragic. Psychoanalysis then becomes the exploration of each person's tragic condition rather than its cure, which (like the satisfaction of desire) is an impossibility. Desire appeals to Lacan because it is the fullest expression of human possibility (though, paradoxically, a never-to-be-realized one). The telos of desire is not pleasure but its transgression. "Pleasure limits the scope of human possibility, the pleasure principle is a principle of homeostasis. Desire, on the other hand, finds its boundary, its strict relation, its limit, and it is in the relation to this limit that it is sustained as such, crossing the threshold imposed by the pleasure principle."[4] The exemplary heroes and heroines of Lacanian psychoanalysis are characters of tragedy like Lear and Antigone, those who have deliberately entered the region of suffering in order to experience the fullest intensity of being.

Freud reveals a tragic vision in *Civilization and Its Discontents* in which he declares that repression is the purchase price of self and civilization. But Freud's tragic vision is qualified by both pessimism and optimism: pessimism in the sense of regret at the unfortunate condition of human life and optimism in the hope that eros will at least provisionally redeem that condition from the curse (?) of its eternal adversary, Thanatos. Lacan, in contrast, purifies psychoanalysis of the contaminations of pessimism and optimism. In doing so, however, he puts the clinical project of psychoanalysis in jeopardy by denying it what would seem to be its aim, indeed, the aim of all clinical practice: the cure of illness.

In fairness to Lacan, it should be said that his view of psychoanalysis as a hermeneutic exercise rather than as a therapy is closer to Freud's original conception of the theoretically interminable character of analysis.[5] The necessary clinical compromise is to assert the possibility of therapeutic progress without claiming the possibility of a cure. Lacan sets himself against all meliorative views of the significance of psychoanalysis.

If not cure, then what? Psychoanalysis teaches the "recognition of 'the validity of suffering' without considering suffering to be intrinsically good."[6] For ego psychology, suffering is an evil that must be avoided, and liberationist theory mutes if it doesn't silence the suffering aspect of desire. Against the received view of the neutrality or impersonality of the analyst, Lacan introduces the idea of the *analyst's* desire. Lacan's desire is not to be normal, but rather to cultivate a "disciplined madness, a divine, but controlled lunacy."[7] Psychoanalysis becomes a clinical practice only for a spiritual elite, those capable of bearing reality.

Lacan, like Nietzsche, believed that life itself is a disease and hence incurable. Freud too shared this view in his theoretical speculations, but he also knew that psychoanalytic practice depended upon a kind of compromise or inhibition of the full implications of psychanalytic theory. Every account of Lacanian practice (in *l'Ècole Freudienne*) testifies to disaster. Could it be otherwise, if the models of fulfillment are the heroic characters of tragedy? It is a rare person who can bear such reality.

In Freud, it is the destructiveness of desire that needs to be repressed. In Lacan, desire is less an active principle than a mode of truth: to repress desire is to avoid knowledge of oneself. Desire is neither biology nor force, it is language and truth. In the spirit of this formulation, Lacan in a reinterpretation of Freud's famous sentence ("Wo es war, soll Ich werden") transfers the site of psychoanalysis from the ego to the id or rather desire. The received interpretation was that of Marie Bonaparte: "Le moi doit deloger le ça," the English version of which is that the ego must dislodge or take over the id. (This becomes a motto for ego psychology.) Lacan translates the sentence in the following manner "where the unconscious subject [Es war! C'était!] was in a locus of being, from there I (Ich) must come to light."⁸ The difference would seem clear and crucial. In the Bonaparte translation, the ego must fortify itself against the destructive assaults of the id; in the Lacanian version, the ego is enriched, expanded, illuminated in the field of unconscious desire. Ego psychologists might protest that they too wish to discover within the field of unconscious desire the ego in order to strengthen it. Lacan would say in response that within the field of desire the unitary ego (which is repressive) weakens and is transformed into a richer plural subject.

Malcolm Bowie acutely notes that the effect of Lacan's "translation" is the opposite of his usual effect upon Freud's writing (". . . What Lacan has done to the sentence, for all his talk of gnomic resonance, is to remove its ambiguity by a route opposite to the one taken by the French translator.")⁹ Moreover, if the context of the sentence matters as it should, Lacan's translation must count as a misreading. The sentence that follows, which would seem to confirm the received version, reads. "It is a work of culture—not unlike the draining of the Zuider Zee."¹⁰ There is elsewhere (in *The Ego and the Id*) sufficient ambiguity in Freud's formulation for Lacan's interpretation to stand as a partial truth.

> As a frontier creature, the ego tries to mediate between the world and the id, to make the id pliable to the world and, by means of its muscular activity, to make the world fall in with the wishes of the id. In point of fact it behaves like the physician during an analytic treatment: it offers itself, with the attention it pays to the real world, as a libidinal object to the id, and aims at attaching the id's libido to itself. It is not only a helper to the id; it is also a submissive slave who courts his master's love. Whenever possible, it tries to remain on good terms with the id; it clothes the id's [unconscious] commands with its [preconscious] rationalizations; it pretends that the id is showing obedience to the admonitions of reality, even when in fact it is remaining obstinate and unyielding; it disguises the id's conflicts with reality and, if possible, its conflicts with the super-ego too. In its position midway between the id and reality, it only too often yields to the temptation to become sycophantic, opportunist and lying, like a politician who sees the truth but wants to keep his place in popular favour.¹¹

But what is desire that it should enrich the subject? It is *not*, Lacan makes clear, "the romantic unconscious of imaginative creation. It is *not* the locus of the divinities of the night."[12] Lacan here acknowledges a truth about the Freudian unconscious that Lawrence treats in his essays on psychoanalysis. And yet the notion of desire as an enrichment suggests something akin to the creative.

Desire, Lacan says again and again, is "the desire of the other." As Bowie has shown, the Other is a protean and treacherous term. "The Other is, for example, now one term in the dialectical couple Subject-Other, now the entire locus or condition of 'otherness' (*alterité, hétéronomie*) that embraces both terms. And the picture is further complicated when the same term is used to bind the intrapersonal and interpersonal worlds together."[13] The ambiguity of Lacan's use of otherness is part of its meaning, not to be resolved.

I want to note, however, that whatever meaning otherness has, it is a condition of alienation, or at least of alienation from the ego. By placing itself in the field of desire, the ego surrenders its freedom to unconscious desire, it invites the compulsions of desire. If unconscious desire was the site of creativity, then alienation would be transformed into inspiration. But Lacan, as we have seen, strictly distinguishes Freudian desire from romantic creativity. It is therefore puzzling that Lacan never addresses the question of the status of desire in relation to freedom or compulsion, though his description of the self's relation to the other suggests alienation and unfreedom.

> All the acts and manifestations which I notice in myself and do not know how to link up with the rest of my mental life must be judged as if they belonged to someone else; they are to be explained by a mental life ascribed to this other period. . . .[14]

> An alien Desire resides at the center of one's being, a Desire whose text is repressed.[15]

Lacan, we must remember, never thought of the alien condition of desire as historically contingent, a cultural misfortune that would ultimately be overcome in some utopian reconciliation with the self. The quarrel between Desire and the Law is eternal and necessary: indeed, Law determines Desire as the basis for action, for without the law, desire would be deprived of its transgressive character.

Desire must "ultimately" be understood as a "system" of verbal representation. It is an open-ended chain of signifiers. It does not come to rest in a final insight, but is an incessant, interminable interpretation of being whose only satisfaction is the process itself. "In the unconscious there is a corpus of knowledge (*un savoir*) which must in no way be conceived as knowledge to be completed, to be closed."[16] Desire in its fullest manifestation is writing itself. If Lacan will be remembered for a single contribution to psychoanalytic thought, it is the idea that the unconscious, synonymous with desire, has the structure of a language, an idea that is only inchoate in the original formulation of Freudian thought. But to state the contribution in this manner misses its dynamic aspect. Structure suggests the fixed and the closed; but the unconscious is in perpetual motion, characterized by discontinuities (leaps over gaps), digressions, simultaneous movement in a variety of directions and its medium is language in all its polyvalence.

It should hardly surprise the reader of Lacan to discover that his main audience is a literary one, for the Lacanian subject—or more accurately Lacanian desire—is ultimately the matter of literature, specifically a modernist literature that specializes in the disrupted narrative, the resistances to origins and closure, a hermetic and opaque rhetoric, and a bewildering polyvalent language. It is a literature whose apotheosis is not Proust with whom Lacan is often compared, but the Joyce of *Ulysses* and *Finnegans Wake.*

There is no reason for us to accept at face value that his prose speaks the unconscious. The enigmatic, the difficult, the abstract may express unconscious thought, but they are not inextricably and exclusively tied to it; they may be functions of *conscious* discourse as well. How do we know—by what signs can we tell—that Lacan's prose represents Lacan's unconscious? And what relation does Lacan's unconscious and its linguistic expression have (assuming that we can establish the prose as that of unconscious desire) to those of others (an essential question, since an act of communication is necessary if he is to persuade us that he possesses the truth of desire)? Surely, Lacan (as a Freudian) would not invoke the idea of a collective unconscious. Lacan does not establish the connection between his unconscious and that of his listeners or readers: indeed, he prides himself on his incommunicability. Lacan's communication exists paradoxically in the charisma that may arise from the hermetic—from the appeal to a portentous mystery.

Most expositions of Lacan come to rest in the revelation of his literary achievement, in a kind of satisfaction that Lacan's true home is literature. Such satisfaction strikes me as problematic. It ignores the relationship of writing itself to repression. Can desire be identified with or reduced to language? Bowie suggests the difficulties, without fully realizing their implications, when he draws an analogy between an externally imposed political censorship and the unconscious censorship that marks all writing: "erasures, blanks and disguises." Bowie remarks with a mixture of admiration and misgiving.

> What Lacan has done by way of his compacted linguistic metaphors is restore to the unconscious materials upon which psychoanalysis operates an Edenic continuity and fullness quite belied by other elements of his argument in "Fonction et Champ." He has deprived both writing and the unconscious considered as writing of their endemic blanks and has alluded neither to the psychoanalytic dialogue nor to the silences that punctuate and propel it.[17]

Lacan's linguistic plenitude entails a full recovery (or a recovery as full as possible) of the field of desire. Bowie implies a possible falsification or misrepresentation in the failure to respect the erasures, blanks, etc. These blanks, erasures, and disguises signify an expanse of desire unavailable to language, or of which language is only a partial sublimation, a displacement.

The Lacanian discovery of the linguistic structure of desire may be in part an expression of a Gallic piety about the ultimacy of discourse. It could be argued (with respect to Foucault as well as Lacan) that the privileging of discourse has the effect of weakening the category of repression, since it makes it very difficult, if not impossible, to distinguish between what is repressed and what is expressed. Such a view is consistent, for instance, with Lacan's rejection of R. D. Laing's distinction between a true self and false self and his more general repudiation of separations between inside and outside.[18]

I speak of the weakening of the category of repression because Lacan cannot, nor does he wish to, destroy all barriers, separations, distinctions. The Real remains Other to the Imaginary and the Symbolic, though the boundaries that separate the three regions may be fluid. In a sense, desire is always paradoxically (for Lacan) both the real and the unreal. It is real in that it is the site of unconscious life, always directed toward the real and in touch (?) with it. At the same time, "desire is the proof of a real Castration which destined the human subject—as a species of metonymy— to take on its fuller meaning only within a signifying chain of narcissistic investments and repressed words."[19] Desire is thus cut off from fulfillment in the real.

Lacan's conception of insatiable desire, forever and of necessity removed from the Real, recalls Proust's conception of desire. Trapped in a linguistically determined realm of desire, all relationships are necessarily played out within language. Thus, for example, the child never experiences directly (in an immediate [Real] way) the authority of a particular father, but rather the *name* of the father, the Law. We can see here once again how inimical Lacan is to the utopian project of a Marcuse or a Deleuze, because utopianism simply denies the *incorrigible* separation of Desire from the Real.

The possibility not contemplated in this singular conception of desire is of a range of *desires* (some satisfiable, others not) and perhaps, more important, the capacity of desires to change reality, to make the Real or portions of it appropriable by the subject. Between the Lacanians and the liberationists, we are left no alternative to tragedy and utopia.

What Lacan finally provides us with, I think, is a new aestheticism, cunningly, though not critically, presented in Shoshana Felman's recent exposition of his work. In distinguishing between earlier psychoanalytic treatments of Edgar Allen Poe's work (in particular those of Joseph Wood Krutch and Marie Bonaparte) and that of Lacan, Felman notes the essential difference in Lacan's attitude toward "the status of the poet" in psychoanalytic discourse. The occasion for the discussion is Lacan's "treatment" of *The Purloined Letter*. Rather than look for the hidden pathological "meaning" of Poe's work, which is supposed to reflect Poe's personal pathology, Lacan looks at the displacements of the signifier on the surface of the tale (Dupin found the letter in the most obvious place). The power of the tale, its "secret," is on the surface, what the poet has given to us, not in a superior grasp of the truth by the demystifying reader-critic.

> . . . the status of the poet is no longer that of the sick patient but, if anything, that of the analyst. . . . The clear-cut opposition between madness and health, or between doctor and patient, is unsettled by the odd functioning of the purloined letter of the unconscious, which no one can possess or master.[20]

Lacan denounces "the reactionary principle" in ego psychoanalysis which assumes "the duality of the one who suffers and the one who cures."[21]

To be a poet analyst is not to be calm and disinterested, the normative emotions of the orthodox analyst, but to be possessed by the hysteria of poetic inspiration. "The discourse of hysteria is closest to the discourse of analysis" and "hysteria is the failed attempt to keep in touch with the dead."[22] Is it a distortion of Lacan's project to say that in his hands the psychoanalytic becomes the poetic imagination, the very medium of desire? The contemporary prestige of desire may blunt our sensitivity to the price paid for a devotion to it. "The road to desire does not pass through *agape* or *philia* or *caritas* . . . these forms of love can cure you of desire."[23] The desire for a cure for Lacan is anathema. The only "cure" that Lacan contemplates is death.

Death is Lacan's richest and most enigmatic subject. And it is many things. It is the refutation of the priority or ascendancy of sexual desire: nothing is more problematic than the satisfaction of sexual desire for Lacan.

> When Freud maintains that sexual desire is at the heart of human desire, all his followers believe him, believe him so strongly that they persuade themselves that it's all so very simple, and that all there remains to do with it is science, the science of sexual desire. It would suffice to remove the obstacles, and it should work all by itself. . . .
>
> But the fact is, it doesn't work. At this point—the turning point—it is said that the subject resists. Why? Because Freud has said so. But one has not understood what it means to *resist*

any more than one has understood the meaning of sexual *desire.*[24]

Death is "the ultimate acceptance and endorsement of one's destiny, the acknowledgment of responsibility for the discourse of the Other in oneself, as well as the forgiving of the discourse."[25] Death is, most puzzlingly of all, "the eternalization [not the satisfaction] of desire." It is a coming to terms with the meaning of life. Such is the ultimacy, the tragic disposition of Lacan's vision that nothing else will do. "Life does not want to heal,"[26] Lacan declares categorically, thus rendering all the particular historical and social forms of life that have tried to change the human condition for the better useless.

In my view, Lacan's powerful view of the Freudian narrative needs to be modified. Desire is the motor of Freudian narrative, and it is in pursuit of a fulfillment that forever eludes it. In this respect, it is like interpretation which seeks to understand but never completes the task of understanding. For Freud only death completes the story, not a catastrophic, externally imposed death, but one that results from the complete exhaustion of life (of the sexual instincts as well as the ego instincts), from, in other words, the generic human will to die, as Keats put it, "to cease upon the midnight of no pain." This view creates problems for the conception of psychoanalysis as a cure. Cure suggests closure, the end of the story, but if the story never really ends, then cure may be an impossibility. Therapy is the term of compromise, the amelioration, but not the elimination of suffering. Lacan is right to stress Freud's essentially tragic spirit, but he fails, I think, to appreciate Freud's conception of conflict. Like the utopians of desire, though from different motives, Lacan resolves the conflict in favor of desire.

In *Civilization and Its Discontents* Freud provides the modern self with its largest stage, and this is the story he tells. Its individuation from its primordial origins creates the condition for conflict within the self and between self and culture for which there is no resolution: how different from *The Secret Sharer! Civilization and Its Discontents* is a tragic story with only a glimmer of hope at the end. Freud postulates an eternal struggle between Eros and Thanatos, mythical characters who represent life and death, respectively. The hope consists in the eternal possibility of eros which, however, can never completely triumph. The book concludes with the following passage:

> Men have gained control over the forces of nature to such an extent that with their help they would have no difficulty in exterminating one another to the last man. They know this, and hence comes a large part of their current unrest, their unhappiness and their mood of anxiety. And now it is to be expected that the other of the two "Heavenly Powers," eternal Eros, will make an effort to assert himself in the struggle with his equally immortal adversary. But who can foresee with what success and with what result?

Freud's narrative proposes no resolution of the conflict, no solace of closure. *Civilization and Its Discontents* is a story about the limits of therapy, the ultimate incurability of the human condition.

In order to appreciate the force of this as a story, we need to realize its difference from the master narrative of the culture he had inherited. That narrative is the story of the return home. We find versions of it in the Bible, for instance, in the story of the Prodigal Son, who leaves his father and squanders his fortune (as Adam squandered Paradise), only to return after the ordeal of loss and estrangement to his home and reconcile himself with his father. The circular pattern of departure and return is the larger pattern of the Bible itself: we find it in the promise of the return to the land of Israel in the Hebrew Bible and of salvation in the New Testament. *Paradise Lost* is a prelude to *Paradise Regained*. In classical antiquity, we have Odysseus' return to Ithaca after long wandering.

Nineteenth-century Hegelian philosophy reveals a similar structure. Hegel's dialectic is in essence a secular reworking of the scriptural parable of the Prodigal Son. Like the parable, Hegel's story is of a historical journey which assumes a beginning (an origin) and conclusive return (i.e., reconciliation) after a middle period of conflict and suffering. The story begins with a vulnerable plenitude, unfolds through loss, separation, and emptiness only to recover a greater and more secure sense of fullness and harmony. The story may move through a series of reconciliations, each vulnerable to further division and conflict, with a final reconciliation in which the dialectic resolves the contradictory elements that have entered into its process.

Freud's narrative is a story of conflicting dualities, ego and id, ego and superego, life against death, Eros against Thanatos, involving temporary accommodations but no permanent resolution. Since the story takes place within the psyche, it is a story of a divided self. The division and inner conflict are without end. The only true closure is death itself. Freud's narrative is an exemplary modernist one, without illusions of progress to some ideal state, without belief in a future redemption. It is realistic, atheistic, though filled with a humane hope that the worst can be averted. The optimistic narrative of psychoanalytic cure in a sense contradicts the narrative of interminable human suffering and struggle. It is the tragic narrative rather than the therapy that is, I think, most congenial to modernist writers.

How do we explain the emergence of this narrative of unresolvable conflict, versions of which we find in the narratives of other modernist writers? The answer, I think, lies in the discovery or recovery of unconscious instinctual life from the repressions of Victorian culture. The nineteenth-century drive toward synthesis, its deep fear and intolerance of conflict belongs, I think, to the repressive ethos of Victorian culture, even when it presents itself in a revolutionary Marxist guise, for example. In recovering the repressed energies of psychic life, Freud did not propose a new regime in the name of those energies: he was not a utopian of the libido like his self-described disciples, Herbert Marcuse and Norman O. Brown. In bringing those energies to the surface Freud did not cancel the repressive terms; rather, he divided the world between them, envisaging an eternal Manichean conflict which would be resolved only by death.

Freud's narrative is distinguished from the nineteenth-century narrative by its realism about the explosive energies of unconscious life and from the postmodern anti-narrative by its ethical impulse to make and sustain a world. In the nineteenth century narrative realism gives way to an ethical utopianism and in the postmodern narrative a passive realism consumes the ethical impulse. Realism and the ethical drive achieve an equilibrium of tension in Freud's thought, which I think is the source of Freud's intellectual and moral authority in modern culture.

154

Freud's narrative is at once realistic and ethical. The nineteenth century repressed reality on behalf of a progressivist notion of a unity and wholeness that would reconcile self to self, self to world, but this utopian reconciliation concealed a repressive project. The postmodern, having inherited the knowledge of repression, has surrendered to a mistrust of the shaping ethical will. Freud recovers the explosive energies that disrupt the old story, the shapeliness of beginning, middle, and end; nevertheless, he holds on to the impulse to constitute a coherent narrative—though not at the expense of truth.

Freud retains what I might call the traditional narrative conception in his desire for the triumph of eros, the sexually inspired wish to constitute a world based on love and harmony. That wish Freud knew could never be permanently satisfied but, as the ending of *Civilization and Discontents* suggests, it is a necessary and humane desire. This knowledge is missing from Lacan. In the previous chapter, I referred to Freud's view of the storyteller's directive influence in his or her "guid[ing] the current of our emotions, dam[ming] it up in one direction and mak[ing] it flow in another." Freud's highest praise of the storyteller is that "he often obtains a great variety of effects from the same material." The American psychoanalyst Roy Schafer makes the therapeutic case for psychoanalytic narrative by stressing narrative desire, the power of narration through the words it uses to describe events in order to direct the analysand's will in benign directions. In an example that Schafer provides, an analysand's initial story about his inability to concentrate on his work and his consequent sense of failure becomes through the interpretive agency of the analyst a story about a man whose lack of concentration reflects an openness of feeling about "girls, . . . my dead father . . . all the failures of my life, etc." Schafer comments: "The narrative has changed from the conscious one of helplessness and failure . . . to a narrative of unconscious activity in another kind of reality. The new story, told now by a more reliable narrator, is a story of personal action and as such it may serve as a basis for change."[27] Concentration means repression; lack of concentration openness to change. Freud sees both the insatiability of desire and the meliorist possibility of a finite and provisional satisfaction of desires, Schafer's new story.

The postmodernist narrative does not only inherit the view of a divided self; it also multiplies the division into fragments and loses even the desire for coherence and wholeness. Indeed, narrative disintegrates in the valorizing of fragmentation, discontinuity, and randomness. For all its talk about desire, the contemporary imagination is bound to Thanatos, not Eros. The telos of its version of desire is death, not love.

It is the desire for coherence and wholeness under the aegis of eros that Lionel Trilling must have had in mind when he remarked on what he perceived as the failure of psychoanalysis to command credence, and he attributed it to the loss of authority that narrative had suffered. Our postmodern epistemology and aesthetic of ungovernable randomness and discontinuity, of a disbelief in origins and mistrust of closure would seem to reflect a deeply anti-narrative bias. I suspect, however, that the epistemology and the aesthetic are more programmatic and ideological than real, that the impulse toward narrative is too deeply human to be extinguished.

Freud's theory or story is about struggle or conflict, unresolvable conflict. Freud's life was a struggle with the intellectually repressive forces that resisted his discoveries. He struggled with himself to contain his anger and disappointments so that he could continue his pursuit of knowledge. Freud's characterization of Moses is probably closer to a self-portrait than it is to an exegesis of Michelangelo's intentions. Conflict is the essence of drama, indeed of narrative. The open-ended story of conflict that Freud tells between ego and id, between ego and superego, Eros and Thanatos, life and death has, I think, an epic dimension, which no modern novel has equaled. We do not think of the heroic and the modern as companions, but Freud's imagination had a heroic aspect. It is no accident that the figure of the ancient Oedipus loomed so large in his work and in the thoughts he had about his own achievement. The modern sensibility can neither endure nor transcend suffering through struggle: it requires the anodyne of therapy, the avoidance of suffering. Freud knew this and he bequeathed Freudian therapy to modernity. What he knew to be beyond the modern was his own heroic capacity for struggle.

8. ❧ "Postmodern" Meditations on the Self: The Work of Philip Roth and Don DeLillo

Two contemporary American writers, Philip Roth and Don DeLillo, provide striking perspectives on the postmodern career of desire, selfhood, and the relations or identity between writing and living. In the stunning conclusion to Philip Roth's novel *The Counterlife* (1986), the novelist-hero Nathan Zuckerman repudiates realist piety by defining his identity as "one long performance and the very opposite of what is thought of as *being oneself.*" A novelist or character of a person in life does not discover a self; he invents it through roles that may not cohere. The unified self is sheer illusion: "To imagine themselves being themselves, living their own real, authentic, or genuine life, has for them [self-aware people] all the aspects of a hallucination." Zuckerman's theory of the self proceeds from the perception that some people are "divided in themselves," a condition that "the whole Western idea of mental health" tries to redeem by establishing an ideal of

"congruity between your self-consciousness and your natural being."
And here again Zuckerman challenges the realist assumption of "a
natural being, an irreducible self. . . . If there even *is* a natural
being, an irreducible self, it is rather small, I think, and may even
be the root of all impersonation—the natural being may be the
skill itself, the innate capacity to impersonate." Zuckerman is then
reduced to the sentiment "that I, for one, have no self. . . . What
I have instead is a variety of impersonations I can do, and not only
of myself—a troupe of players that I have internalized, a permanent company of actors that I can call upon when a self is required,
an ever-evolving stock of pieces and parts that forms my reper-
toire."*

Zuckerman's excursus into the theory of self turns out to be
an exercise in wooing back his estranged wife, who had more than
she could take of his compulsive Jewish life, his "paranoid" obsessions with the anti-Semitism of English gentry: "Come back and
we'll play with [our subjectivities] together. We could have great
times as Homo Ludens and wife, inventing the imperfect future.
We can pretend to be anything we want. All it takes is impersonation" (C, 321). Opposed to this ludic and liberating dream of
desire is a counterimagination of desire in its actuality as a ruthless
tyrant over which its victim, the possessed self, has no control:
Zuckerman speaks of "the terrible unruliness spawned by uncon-
strainable desire—the plotting, the longing, the crazily impetuous
act, the dreaming relentlessly of the other" (C, 6). And elsewhere,
he characterizes his alter-ego brother Henry as being "in crazy
flight . . . from the folly of sex, from the intolerable disorder of
virile pursuits and the indignities of secrecy and betrayal, from the
enlivening anarchy that overtakes anyone who even sparingly
abandons himself to uncensored desire" (C, 132), a despairing view
that recalls the scenes of desire in Mann and Ford.

Both the ludic and the destructive play themselves out in imagination, but imagination is no longer "the bounded space of composition." It is no coincidence that in his recent work, *The Counterlife*, in the directly autobiographical *The Facts*, and in *Deception*,
the boundaries between writing and living become fluid, con-

* Philip Roth, *The Counterlife* (New York: Farrar, Straus and Giroux, 1986), pp.
319–21. Subsequent references have been indicated with the abbreviation C and the
page number.

fused and confusing for narrator and reader alike. In *The Counter-life*, it becomes impossible to disentangle art and life. Sexual impotence is "like an artist's life drying up for good" (*C*, 35). "A life of writing books is a trying adventure in which you cannot find out where you *are* unless you lose your way" (*C*, 131). There is no life beyond writing, or no life that is not absorbed by the novelist whose days are spent at the writing table, no adventure that has an autonomous existence outside his imagination. "The treacherous imagination is everybody's maker—we are all the invention of each other. . . . We are all each other's authors" (*C*, 145). The famous carnality of Roth's characters is now *"really* a fiction" (*C*, 184). But if life itself is a fiction, "the bounded space of composition" that the modernists assumed no longer exists.

In *The Facts*, which Roth wrote as a therapeutic antidote to a nervous collapse, the distinction between fact and fiction, between the real and the imaginative has eroded, if not disappeared. The "I" of an autobiography is as much a character, a structure constituted by language as the first or third person in a fictional narrative; the sequence of events in an autobiography is as much a narrative construction as the sequence of events in a novel. Roth knows this.

> I recognize that I'm using the word "facts" here, in this letter, in its idealized form and in a much more simpleminded way than is meant in its title. Obviously the facts are never just coming at you but are incorporated by an imagination that is formed by your previous experience. There is something naive about a novelist like myself talking about presenting himself "undisguised" and depicting "life without fiction."*

If autobiography and the self are a textual construction, we cannot simply identify autobiography with living and fiction with writing. If there is a difference between autobiography and fiction for Roth, it is the difference between self-justification and extenuation, on the one hand, and self-evisceration, on the other. "Your medium for really merciless self-evisceration, your medium for genuine self-confrontation is me" (*F*, 185), Zuckerman tells his author in a letter that follows *The Facts*. Zuckerman is scathing about what the autobiography lacks.

* Philip Roth, *The Facts: A Novelist's Autobiography* (Penguin, 1988), p. 8. Subsequent references have been indicated with the abbreviation *F* and the page number.

In this book you are not permitted to tell what it is you tell best: kind, discreet, careful—changing people's names because you're worried about hurting their feelings—no, this isn't you at your most interesting. (*F*, 162).

Without all the exigencies of a full-scale, freewheeling narrative to overwhelm the human, if artistically fatal, concern for one's vulnerable self, you are incapable of admitting that you were more responsible for what befell you than you wish to recall. (*F*, 175)

Here you investigate virtually nothing of a serious sexual nature and somewhat astonishingly, seem almost to indicate that sex has never really compelled you. (*F*, 183)

Zuckerman only confirms what we come to suspect: that the risk-taking violence of the imagination, its acting out of desire, makes it therapeutically unsound. It may be that the inhibitions that constrain the autobiography enabled Roth to overcome his psychological turmoil. Zuckerman advises Roth not to publish *The Facts*. Fortunately, Roth did not follow the advice, because the interest of the autobiography goes beyond its therapeutic function; it illuminates in its very deficiencies Roth's imaginative relation to the world or perhaps more accurately his relation to the imagination.

Roth turned to autobiography because he felt trapped in the life that he had been living, the life of imagination. In *The Counterlife*, the novel that precedes *The Facts*, Roth discovered the possibility of alternative lives that can be lived by a particular self. *The Facts* pursues the implications of this discovery. Addressing Zuckerman, Roth declares: "If while writing I couldn't see exactly what I was up to, I do now: this manuscript embodies *my* counterlife, the antidote and answer to all those fictions that culminated in the fiction of you. If in one way *The Counterlife* can be read as fiction about structure, then this is the bare bones, the structure of a life without the fiction" (*F*, 9).

Roth's apologia is paradoxical, for it reverses what we think of as the usual process. We consider the facts ("jottings in a notebook" as Roth calls them) as representing the life and the fictions as the counterlife, that is, alternative imaginings of lived experience, a kind of liberation from the prison house of experience.

But has Roth given us merely "the bare bones," as he tells Zuckerman? Zuckerman's wife Maria finds Roth's autobiography to be an "extraordinarily coherent narrative," which depresses her. And what determines the coherence is, of course, not the intrinsic logic of the events as they occurred but Roth's retrospective imposition of an order, which is meant to explain what had become of Roth, how his life had delivered him to the nervous breakdown that he suffered in 1987. What emerges is an image of Roth as a very ordinary, indeed drab human being. In the words of Maria: "I don't mean that he's presenting a deceptive image to make himself look terrific, . . . he looks to me awfully narrow. and driven and, my God so pleasureless" (*F*, 190). What vexes Zuckerman and his wife is the absence of qualities and energies in Roth's ordinary life that we find in the fiction: the fierce sexuality, the aggression toward self and others—in short, the violence and extremity of Roth's imagination. "Caprice [Roth writes in *Deception*] is at the heart of a writer's nature. Exploration, fixation, isolation, verism, fetishism, austerity, levity, perplexity, childishness, *et cetera*. The nose in the seam of the undergarment—*that's* the writer's nature. *Im*purity."[1] But this is not the whole story. *The Facts* reveals, as the novels do not, the life destructive power of imagination and its irresistible temptation for Roth.

The deepest enigma in the autobiography is Roth's incredibly destructive marriage to Josie. The marriage is the fact that becomes the occasion for the imaginative transformations of *When She Was Good* and *My Life as a Man*. Why, knowing as Roth knew, before his marriage that Josie was a hysterical liar, needy, demanding, paranoid, does he decide to marry her anyway? The autobiography discloses the answer not to be found in the novels. "The question is how could I resist her. . . . How could I be anything *but* mesmerized by this overbrimming talent for brazen self-invention, how could a half-formed, fledgling novelist hope ever to detach himself from this undiscouragable imagination unashamedly concocting the most diabolical ironies? It wasn't only she who wanted to be indissolubly joined to my authorship and my book but I who could not separate myself from hers" (*F*, 111).

The self-invention to which Roth refers was her feigning pregnancy by purchasing a urine specimen from a pregnant black woman for a couple of dollars, taking money from Roth for an abortion (as a condition for his marrying her), then concocting in a vivid and persuasive way (tears, uncontrollable shivering) "the horrible medical details of the humiliating procedure" (*F*, 111). The time of the supposed abortion was spent watching the Susan Hayward melodrama, *I Want to Live!*

Of course, Roth could not possibly know the details of Josie's inventiveness when he agreed to marry her, so the fact of the inventiveness is retrospective, and therefore hardly the cause of the marriage. Roth means to understand his attraction to Josie as an attraction to her demonic imaginative quality, the facts of her "abortion" being only confirmatory. The autobiography is the ordinary (actual) life of the writer in which demonic and imaginative characters like Josie act out their destructive careers, "redeemed" only by the capacity of fiction to reenact the demons in the novelist's imagination.

The autobiography is a grim satire on the temptations of the imagination: its power is associated with the grotesque, the obscene, the painful. The distinctive virtue of the autobiography is not its truthfulness, but its coherent ordinariness through which we can perceive the frightening temptations of the extraordinary. *The Facts* tells us what we may have sensed but not fully realized that for Roth the fictional imagination is the opposite of the therapeutic. The imagination eviscerates, it does not heal.

Why does Roth, knowing how terrible it is, succumb to the imagination? For Roth the imagination is a god. In *Deception* Roth pursues what has become his obsessive argument that the imagination's obligation to its own freedom, or perhaps more accurately, to its own necessity is greater than its obligation to the real. Roth suffers from an inferiority complex. For all his talent and lucidity he feels threatened by his ordinariness. In the sixties he had written that American reality exhibited an extravagant imagination (he had characters like Joseph McCarthy, Roy Cohn, and Charles Van Doren in mind) that surpassed the writer's imagination. How could he hope to compete? In *The Facts* he speaks of his account of Maureen's "pregnancy" in *My Life as a Man* as exactly parallel to the facts of Josie's. "Those scenes represent one of the few occasions when I haven't spontaneously set out to improve on actuality in the interest of being more interesting—I couldn't have been *as* interesting" (*F*, 107). Imagination in our secular society represents the effort to transcend our ordinariness. And grace in the modern novelist's world from Henry James to the present is being *interesting*.

But what does it mean to be interesting? Josie embodies "interesting" in an exemplary way.

> To reshape even its smallest facet would have been an aesthetic blunder, a defacement of her life's single great imaginative feat, that wholly original act which freed her from the fantasied role as my "editor" to become, if for a moment only, a literary rival of audacious flair, one of those daringly "pitiless" writers of the kind Flaubert found most awesome, the sort of writer my own limited experience and orderly development prevented me then from even beginning to resemble—masterly pitilessness was certainly nowhere to be found in the book of stories whose publication she so envied and to which she was determined to be allied. In a fifteen-page explanation of human depravity by one of his garrulous, ruined, half-mad monologists, Dostoevsky himself might not have been ashamed to pay a hundred-word tribute to the ingenuity of that trick. (*F*, 107)

The novelist must be able to endure the most searing experience, to have a mind of steel, to be pitiless. "Masterly pitilessness" Roth calls it, and typically he envies it in the great masters (Flaubert, for example) "the sort of writer my own limited experience and orderly development prevented me from becoming." In this episode, Roth congratulates himself on having demonstrated a comparable capacity: "My imaginative faculties had managed to outlive the waste of all that youthful strength" (*F*, 108).

The relationship between autobiography and fiction is the reverse of what one might expect. Autobiography is not simply the representation of facts, it is the relentless shaping of them in the light of the writer's present understanding of what he has become. Only the fictional imagination can liberate the facts from the tyranny of present understanding, free them from teleology. Autobiography is narrative with a vengeance, hostile to the anarchy of randomness. Zuckerman's wife Maria, quoted in his letter to Roth, reminds us of the centrifugal powers of the modernist and postmodernist fictional imagination.

> "Nothing is random. Not that what happens to him has no point. Nothing that he says happens to him in his life does not get turned into something that is useful to him. Things that

appear to have been pointlessly destructive and poisoning, things that look at the time to have been wasteful and appalling and spoiling, are the things that turn out to be, say, the writing of *Portnoy's Complaint*. As each person comes into his life, you begin to think, 'So what is this person's usefulness going to be? What is this person going to provide him in the way of a book?' Well, maybe this is the difference between a writer's life and an ordinary life." "Only the subject," I said, "is his formative experiences as a writer. Randomness is not the subject—that's *Ulysses*." "Yes, the facts, as far as he's concerned as a writer, have to do with who he is as a writer. But there are lots and lots of other facts, all the stuff that spins around and is not coherent or *important*. This is just such an extraordinarily, relentlessly coherent narrative, that's all. . . ." (*F*, 189–90)

Josie's "usefulness" is to propel his imagination beyond the *ordinariness* of experience. The drama of *The Facts* (confirmed by the framing letters) is the conflict between the Roth's need for ordinariness and his desire for the imaginatively extraordinary: for the life of desire. Roth lives in the condition of ambivalence. He is compelled and threatened by demonic imagination. It fulfills, but does not console him. Autobiography is therapy, imagination is transcendence. By trying to turn the facts of his life into meaning, by achieving a narrative control of events, writing restores purpose to life. The paradox results when Roth moves to liberate himself from mere ordinary purposiveness into the ferocious space of imagination. Roth is scrupulous in not romanticizing the temptations of the imagination.

Desire performs its imperial role in the cinematic consumerist culture in which we live. Among contemporary writers no one has imagined and understood it more impressively than Don DeLillo.

DeLillo would endorse Roth's view of the self as a nullity, but he would, I think, object to the theatrical metaphor. At least one of his characters, Lyle, the astronaut hero of *Players*, speaks of being bored by "three-dimensional bodies" in the theater, because they produce in him a kind of "torpor." He prefers "the manipulated depth of film."* Could it be that Roth's use of the theatrical

* Don DeLillo, *Players* (New York: Knopf, 1974), p. 100. Subsequent references in the text have been indicated with the abbreviation *P* and the page number.

metaphor betrays an unsurmounted attachment to the substantial (three-dimensional) self? DeLillo's role players, in any case, have been completely emptied of substance. *Players* concludes with a striking image of the empty or emptying self, more radical and more convincing than what seems to me the desperate effort of Roth's alter ego to disburden himself of the guilts and sufferings that, alas, constitute his self. Here is the concluding paragraph of *Players:*

> The propped figure, for instance, is barely recognizable as male. Shedding capabilities and traits by the second, he can still be described (but quickly) as well-formed, sentient and fair. We know nothing else about him. (*P*, 111)

"But quickly" because he is already disappearing as he is described. This disembodied, disappearing self is a function of DeLillo's cinematic imagination. The screen is a two-dimensional space. Its quintessential subject, the cartoon character, appears and disappears in the blink of an eye. Pulverized, mashed, flattened, the cartoon character can be restored to its original dignity at a moment's notice. In a sense, even the human subjects of films have the characterless malleability of the cartoon subject, insofar as they are subject to the most incredible transformations and possess no center of resistance to cinematic change. Film is the medium par excellence of resistance-less change; anything our heart desires can happen, because there is nothing of substance, of sufficient weight and density to prevent it from happening. The movie screen provides a mirror in which we learn to transform ourselves, to play a variety of roles at will.

The consciousness of Lyle, the central male character of *Players,* is capable of turning into a split screen in which he sees himself simultaneously "as a former astronaut who walked on the surface of the moon" and "as a woman interviewing the astronaut in a TV studio." The "astronaut persona" is particularly telling, because it involves "weightlessness as a poetic form of anxiety and isolation" (*P*, 108), the screen itself being the very medium of weightlessness. This weightless, kinetic medium in turn reveals the monetary essence of our culture:

> He'd seen the encoding rooms, the microfilming of checks, money moving, shrinking as it moved, beginning to elude visualization,

> to pass from a paper existence to electronic sequences. . . . Lyle thought of his own money not as a medium of exchange but as something to be consigned to data storage, traceable only through magnetic flashes. (*P*, 110)

Lyle's experience of money as magnetic flashes has an uncanny resemblance to his watching television. His main pleasure is "the tactile-visual delight of switching channels, . . . transforming even random moments of content into pleasing territorial abstractions" (*P*, 16). Throughout the novel, the switching of scenes, the play of dialogue between characters or within a single consciousness (the back and forth switching of voices) takes precedence over the plot, however dramatic its potential. Like DeLillo's other books, *Players* is full of melodramatic promise, a terrorist plot to blow up the stock exchange, adulterous affairs, a particularly gruesome suicide by fire, but the promise of plot is not meant to be kept; it is subordinated to "territorial abstraction."

It is precisely the power and the desire of the cinematic medium to present *spectacular* instances of experiences, to uncover the extreme and make us feel that it represents the totality of our lives. Indeed, to the extent that we live in the cinematic world (some households have television sets in every room) our lives become the lives of cinematic representation, as in this instance of what I would call the cinematic real from *Players:*

> She couldn't fall asleep. The long ride was still unraveling in her body, tremors and streaks. She turned on the black-and-white TV, the one in the bedroom. An old movie was on, inept and boring, fifties vintage. There was a man, the hero, whose middle-class life was quietly coming apart. First there was his brother, the black sheep, seriously in debt, pursued by grade-B racketeers. Phone calls, meetings, stilted dialogue. Then there was his wife, hospitalized, apparently dying of some disease nobody wanted to talk about. In a series of tediously detailed scenes, she was variously brave, angry, thoughtful and shrill. Pammy couldn't stop watching. The cheapness was magnetic. She experienced a new obliteration of self-awareness. Through blaring commercials for swimming pool manufacturers and computer trainee institutes, she remained in the chair alongside the bed. As the movie grew increasingly maudlin, she became more upset. The bus window had become a TV screen filled with serial

grief. The hero's oldest boy began to pass through states of what the doctor called reduced sensibility. He would sit on the floor in a stupor, either unable to speak or refusing to, his limbs immobile. Phone calls from the hero's brother increased. He needed money fast, or else. Another hospital scene. The wife recited from a love letter the hero had written her when they were young.

Pammy was awash with emotion. She tried to fight it off knowing it was tainted by the artificiality of the movie, its plain awfulness. She felt it surge through her, this billowing woe. Her face acquired a sheen. She ran her right hand over the side her head, fingers spread wide. Then it came, onrushing, a choppy sobbing release. She sat there, hands curled at her temples, for fifteen minutes, crying, as the wife died, the boy recovered, the brother vowed to regain his self-respect, the hero in his pleated trousers watched his youngest child ride a pony. (P, 204–5)

The real and the cinematic have become indistinguishable. The deliberate insubstantiality of DeLillo's characters is compensated for by an extraordinary and eloquent plenitude of speech. Characters become meditative voices, capable of extended vatic aphorisms about the world. The meditations serve as a revelation of and a defense against a killer boredom to which our consuming society vainly tries to provide an antidote. The meditation, like this one from DeLillo's first novel, *Americana*, may tell the story of a desiring empty self:

In this country there is a universal third person, the man we all want to be. Advertising has discovered this man. It uses him to express the possibilities open to the consumer. To consume in America is not to buy; it is to dream. Advertising is the suggestion that the dream of entering the third person singular might possibly be fulfilled.[2]

Consuming is dreaming, the deferment of actual consumption, hence the perpetuation of the feeling of emptiness.

In *White Noise* the two main sites of experience and dialogue are the supermarket and the TV screen. Jack Gladney, the protagonist, constantly runs into his friend and colleague Murray Siskind at the supermarket, where they conduct their most serious conver-

DESIRE AND ITS DISCONTENTS

sations about the state of contemporary culture. "This was the fourth or fifth time I'd seen him in the supermarket, which was roughly the number of times I'd seen him on campus."* The soul of American society reveals itself in the supermarket: Siskind affirms "the new austerity, . . . flavorless packaging," which reflects "some kind of spiritual consensus. It's like World War III. Everything is white. They'll take our bright colors away and use them in the war effort" (*WN*, 18). The talk about food is endless and indiscriminate. Pretzels, beer, peanuts, pizzas, popcorn, chocolate, featureless generic food are the objects of both rampant consumerism and serious (and therefore funny) discussion.

What the supermarket gives us is not real food but its facsimile. The food is chemically composed, canned, packaged, advertised: we consume it all. The supermarket (a trope for all sites of consumption) is filled with an abundance of items, but the main staple of that world is not the tangible item, the real thing, but what stimulates and sustains it in an endless deferment.

The cinema, like the supermarket, is where we escape from the humdrum of "reality." It is the locus of desire. A recent book on film has the quintessential title, *The Desire to Desire*. "The twentieth century is on film. It's the filmed century," a character in *The Names* tells us.[3] In a commercial culture dominated by the media and the values of advertising, and in an intellectual culture that textualizes the world and casts doubt about the existence of the real or of our ever being capable of knowing and experiencing it, the cinema (even more than the written text) becomes the place where we "truly live."

Whether in the movie house or on TV, film stimulates desire, arouses our imaginations, but disables our capacity for real experience. It neither satisfies desire nor makes for catharsis. Its effect is anaesthetic. In *White Noise* Siskind speaks of a "car crash in the movies as a celebration, a moment of high spirits and innocence and fun" in which "the crushed bodies, the severed limbs" are irrelevant (*WN*, 218). In the same novel a "nameless Irishman is disturbed by the prospect that the riot or terrorist act which caused his death would not be covered by the media" (*WN*, 194). Not

* Don DeLillo, *White Noise* (New York: Viking, 1986), p. 35. Subsequent references in the text have been indicated with the abbreviation *WN* and the page number.

because, as one might think, the media bestow celebrity, but because they anesthetize the pain of dying.

Our age, we have been told and shown endlessly, is an apocalyptic age. The apocalypse may be the dominant media trope of our time; its endless replay has inured us to the real suffering it might entail. We repeatedly witness the assassination of Kennedy, the mushroom cloud over Hiroshima, the disintegration of the Challenger space shuttle in the sky. Repetition wears away the pain. It also perfects the image or our experience of it. By isolating the event and repeating it, its content, its horror evaporates. What we have before us is its form and rhythm. The event becomes aesthetic and the effect upon us anaesthetic. The cinema does not satisfy insatiable desire, it anaesthetizes it. The phenomenon is sometimes called kitsch.

Kitsch is a difficult word to define. It is a term of contempt for art of little value or an art that is meretricious, a misleading, ingratiating semblance of the real thing. What makes it appealing is its pleasantness, the ease with which the consumer can assimilate it, derive pleasure from it. There are many definitions or characterizations of kitsch, but it can best be grasped by example. Saul Friedländer conceives it as the insipidly decorative: "a branch of mistletoe under the lamps in a railway waiting room, nickled plate glass in a public place, artificial flowers gone astray in Whitechapel, a lunch box decorated with Vosges fir."[4] Kitsch covers over reality with the appearance of art: it appeals to the desire for the pleasant and the harmonious.

There is a special case of kitsch that Friedländer calls "the kitsch of death" that is relevant to the cinematic experiences of DeLillo's characters. Friedländer characterizes it as "a juxtaposition of the kitsch aesthetic and of the themes of death that creates the surprise, that special frisson." Friedländer means violent, catastrophic death. But kitsch and death, it would seem, are incompatible. How then does one achieve "the kitsch of death"? By aestheticizing it through an apocalyptic lyricism: "the livid sky slashed by immense purple reflections, flames surging from cities, flocks and men fleeing toward the glowing horizon,"[5] and, one might add, all confined to the safety of the screen.

DeLillo presents the pervasive experience of kitsch without being complicit with it. Contrast Friedländer's characterization of the kitsch of death with DeLillo's seeing through it in this passage from *White Noise:*

> Ever since the airborne toxic event, the sunsets had become almost unbearably beautiful. Not that there was a measurable connection. If the special character of Nyoden Derivative (added to the everyday drift of effluents, pollutants, contaminants and delirants) had caused this aesthetic leap from already brilliant sunsets to broad towering riddled visionary skyscapes, tinged with dread, no one had been able to prove it. (*WN*, 170)

Beyond the illusions of desire, DeLillo portrays the omnipresence of death.

> Supermarkets this large and clean and modern are a revelation to me. I spent my life in small steamy delicatessens with slanted display cabinets full of trays that hold soft wet lumpy matter in pale colors. High enough cabinets so you had to stand on tiptoes to give your order. Shouts, accents. In cities no one notices specific dying. Dying is a quality of the air. It's everywhere and nowhere. (*WN*, 38)

Jack Gladney, the hero of *White Noise*, is obsessed with the fact of death. He looks at family photos and wonders "who will die first." The question becomes a refrain in the novel. On another occasion he identifies the self with death and asks, given this identification, "how [can the self] be stronger than death?" (*WN*, 30). The cinema offers a solution, by turning people into nonparticipating spectators of destruction. In film, we watch the most spectacular and apocalyptic enactments of death without being personally affected by them. DeLillo's characters (like us) comfortably watch "floods, mud slides, emptying volcanoes," while eating "take out Chinese." "Every disaster made us wish for something bigger, grander, more sweeping" (*WN*, 268). Here DeLillo beautifully exemplifies Friedlander's conception of the "Kitsch of death." ("Take out Chinese" is a splendid touch, the perfect example of kitsch food.) Death and destruction in their cinematic pretenses become objects of desire. DeLillo's characters are fully invested in this cinematic play with destruction and death, but nothing can allay the persistent fear of real dying. Gladney and his wife Babette are terrified by the prospect of dying, hoping to master the fear by consuming a miracle drug Dylar, that (need we be told) turns out be a fraud. The anaesthetic effect wears off.

The cinema does not empower us to confront our mortality; it offers us an escape from the real contemplation of death while enjoying its melodramatic facsimiles. The cinematic imagination at once creates and reveals violence and death. It "says" in effect that I will express, bring to the surface the horror and terror that we repress in order to anaesthetize it. But this is not all. The cinematic world has become "reality."

There is in our cultural life a powerful drive to erase boundaries, to blur genres, to destabilize and subvert distinctions. Our "postmodern" culture has transformed the relations between life and imagination, between living and writing. The cinema has imperialized the world. It has become the main site of desire, but it stimulates desire only to anaesthetize it. In thrall to the images on the screen, the self, having lost its quiddity, dissolves painlessly into those very images.

Is the imperialism of desire and the dissolution of the self an irreversible condition of contemporary life? Only if we accept the currently fashionable view that the self is not a natural fact, but a fictional construction. I would suggest that the opposite is the truth: that the ordinary, experiential self *is* a natural fact, that we intuitively, instinctively experience a sense of identity, or at least the continuity of our identities, and that without the natural sentiment we would go crazy and suffer a radical sense of fragmentation, discontinuity and emptiness. The apocalyptic imagination (whether as writing or cinema) does not imitate reality (the reality of ourselves) but acts against it.

One would expect those who imagine the self as discontinuous and fragmented also to conceive the writing and living as discontinuous. But this is not always the case. The mimetic view persists in the assumption that the fictional conceptions of the self as fragmented and marginal represent the reality of persons. Writing represents not the reality of persons, but the desire to explode the self, to multiply it, to liberate it from the constraints and oppressions of unitariness. If writing merely corresponded to the real self (whether in its continuity or discontinuity), it would be superogatory. Its raison d'être is its inventive and explosive power. The desire of postmodern writing is to perpetuate the disintegration of the self. I take the perpetuation of self-disintegration or multiplication, the resistance to closure as a sign that it need not be confined to the space of writing, that, in other words, self-disintegration is conceived as the process of life itself. But if, as I have tried to argue, the disintegrative imagination of the self is not liberating for life, we are not compelled to submit to the apocalyptic imperative in the name of realism. We are free to distinguish between imagining and living and to protect our sense of the quiddity of our beings.

9
ॐ Desire and the Self

A utopianism of desire persists in the politics of feminism, which opposes desire to patriarchal reason or in gay liberation, which seeks to expand the boundaries of socially permissible desire, not necessarily to eliminate altogether the idea of a boundary. I say "not necessarily" because it is sometimes hard to disentangle fantasies of illimitable desire from the more limited projects of desire. Does desire advance the boundaries, productively expanding the self, or does it declare the very idea of a boundary obsolete?

In *A Room of One's Own*, Virginia Woolf provides us with a basis for making such distinction in her criticism of *Jane Eyre*. She quotes a long passage in chapter 12 in which Jane in effect celebrates her discontent with life. Here is a selection from the passage:

. . . I longed for a power of vision which might overpass the limit; which might reach the busy world, towns, regions, full of life I had heard of but never seen. . . .

Who blames me? Many, no doubt, and I shall be called discontented. I could not help it: the restlessness was in my nature; it agitated me to pain sometimes. . . .

It is vain to say human beings ought to be satisfied with tranquility; they must have action; and they will make it if they cannot find it. . . . Women are supposed to be very calm generally; but women feel just as men feel. . . . It is thoughtless to condemn them, or laugh at them, if they seek to do more or learn more than custom has pronounced necessary for their sex.

When thus alone I not unfrequently heard Grace Poole's laugh. . . .

Virginia Woolf speaks of the sudden reference to the mad woman in the attic "as an awkward break." But doesn't the laugh mock Jane's discontent and its potentiality for madness? Woolf goes on to say that Brontë had "more genius in her than Jane Austen," but that "indignation . . . deformed and twisted" her books.

> She will write in a rage where she should write calmly, she will write foolishly where she should write wisely. She will write of herself where she should write of her character. She is at war with her lot. How could she help but die young, cramped and thwarted?[1]

What Woolf has perceived is that beyond the reasonable desire "to do more or learn more than custom had pronounced necessary for their sex" is a discontent, an insatiable desire that nothing will satisfy and that such desire breeds the resentment that disfigures the imagination itself. The imagination may be the site where insatiable desire "legitimately" plays itself out, but in the instances that we have looked at (Proust, Dostoevsky, Conrad, Brontë, and Mann) the imagination of desire is counterpoised with a cautionary wisdom about its dangers. The writing of desire itself suffers without the accompanying wisdom.

Desire has come to function as an essentialist trope. The concentration of power in any single human energy or faculty, what we might call its ideological formulation of necessity becomes a tyranny over other energies, if it doesn't completely repress them.

174

Foucault's "solution" (about which he himself was pessimistic) is to try to defuse or diffuse power. Power cannot be absolutely destroyed. All mediations or particular expressions of human energies may grant power to one or more of them (reason, morality, freedom, sexuality). The diffusion of power is no more and no less than the provisionality and delimitation of each and every energy. As I have already argued, Foucault's solution *suffers* from a conception of power which leads him to regard it as an unequivocal evil. But Foucault is, I think, right to have dramatized the actual or potential tyranny of each and every discourse, including the discourse of desire. The idea that desire may become tyrannical must seem paradoxical to the many who would identify desire with freedom itself. After all, doesn't everyone dream of having one's desires satisfied? And isn't the thwarting of desire the very definition of unfreedom? As we have seen, however, the profoundest writers about desire conceive of desire under the regime of necessity, not freedom. Foucault's critique is already within a "tradition." Behind him is the work of Nietzsche.

For Nietzsche, a principal source of tyranny is the platonic conviction that of the three sources of human motivation (reason, will, and the appetites) reason should dominate. As Alexander Nehamas puts it, "Having identified a large number of independent motives and character traits, Nietzsche, in contrast to Plato, considers that the question which should govern the self requires a different answer in each particular case."[2] The implication of this view is not confined to reason. If reason is not required in one case, it may indeed be required in another. And if desire is required in one case, it may not be required in another. Moreover, what does it mean for something to be *required*? Does it mean following out what is experienced as the necessity of one's nature, the overwhelming desire for a particular satisfaction, or does it mean achieving control or mastery of the desire as Nietzsche, for instance, envisioned through the exercise of the artistic will? The considerations are complex and even confused, but it is clear that the possibility of tyranny is not confined to the discourse of reason. All discourses are potentially tyrannical.

An extraordinarily powerful instance of the tyranny of desire in the English novelistic tradition is that of Sue Bridehead in Hardy's *Jude the Obscure*. At the moment that he dramatizes the price of the repression of the passion in Victorian society, Hardy with an acute moral intelligence perceives in the character of Sue the potential tyranny of desire, that is of desire turning into a categorical imperative for those who are naturally without passion. Speaking from "experience and unbiased nature," Jude agrees that Sue shouldn't try to overcome her "prudish" sexual aversion for Phillotson and even her reticence with Jude.[3] Later on, Sue speaks of parting as a "natural" state.[4] Nature in Sue is associated not with desire but with its absence, and Hardy's abiding principle is that nature should not be coerced. It is a desecration of life, both Nietzsche and Foucault would agree, to impose an imperative upon those incapable of strong passion just as it is a desecration to repress those of strong passion. (In this perspective, Jane Eyre's "I could not help it" demands a respect that Woolf's and my moralizing does not acknowledge.) We are subject to the necessities of our nature, but we should not be subject to the necessity of someone else's nature—that is, a personal necessity transformed into a universal principle.

Nietzsche tried to imagine the conditions of a life free of the coercions of all the universalizing institutional forms of life: politics, ethics, religion. The alternative for Nietzsche was aesthetic consciousness, with its own kind of tyrannical order. Nietzsche did not object to the orderings of art. On the contrary, he rejected "the assumption that human nature is best expressed in perfect freedom," arguing instead that "all that there is or has been on earth of freedom, subtlety, boldness, dance, masterly sureness, whether in thought itself or in government, or in rhetoric and persuasion, in the arts just as in ethics, has developed only owing to 'the tyranny of such capricious laws.' "

For example, Nietzsche objects not to the "tyranny" of Christianity, but rather to its dogmatism, its concealment of "the fact that its direction is only one direction among many others." He does not mean to promote the kind of rapid changes of fashion that characterizes postmodernity. In fact, he advocates "*obedience* over a long period of time and in *a single* direction; given that, something always develops, and has developed, for whose sake it is worthwhile to live on earth, for example, virtue, art, music, dance, reason, spirituality."[5] Nietzsche's anti-essentialism (his valuing of the complexity of the person and the diversity of persons) does not preclude the possibility of coherence. The coherent person is not a seamless unity, but the representative of the will to self-mastery.

The "natural" self, according to Nietzsche, is neither constant nor stable. In one version (and there are other versions in Nietzsche's thought), the self has no reality beyond the episodes that compose it. The subject is no more than the sum of its deeds, its moods, its ideas. One need not subscribe to this view of the self (I have already argued the contrary view that the quiddity of the self is a phenomenologically experienced fact) to appreciate Nietzsche's response to the heterogeneity of what he understood to be the "natural" self. Through the route of artifice, Nietzsche affirms the necessity of the coherent self. Unlike many postmodernists, he does not rest content with a heterogeneous random subjectivity. The heterogeneity of the self constitutes a challenge to the artistic will to create a harmony: "An admirable self consists of a large number of powerful and conflicting tendencies that are controlled and harmonized."[6] Through the route of artifice, Nietzsche affirms the necessity of the coherent self. The tyranny that Nietzsche repudiates is not the aesthetic order that constitutes one's personality, an order that is subject to change according to the necessities of one's nature, but the alien imposition of an external order that dogmatically declares itself universal and eternal. Is it not the case that Desire, reified and abstract, has become such an alien order or, should we say, disorder?

?~ Notes

Introduction: What We Talk About When We Talk About Desire

1. Leo Bersani, *A Future for Astyanax: Character and Desire in Literature* (Berkeley: University of California Press, 1977), p. ix.

2. Julia Kristeva, *Desire in Language*, translated by Thomas Gora, Alice Jardine, and Leon S. Roudiez (New York: Columbia University Press, 1980), p. 23.

3. The early modern philosophers of desire (Hume and Nietzsche) did not conceive of desire as freedom. They viewed it as a determinism, and their conceptions were pluralistic. Hume, for instance, envisaged contentions between desires in which one desire might overcome another, reason being relegated to an instrumental role.

4. Roland Barthes, *A Lover's Discourse* (New York: Hill and Wang, 1978), p. 174.

5. Barthes, *A Lover's Discourse*, p. 55.

6. Barthes, *A Lover's Discourse*, p. 212.

7. Jane Gallop, *Reading Lacan* (Ithaca: Cornell University Press, 1985), p. 104.

8. Serge Doubrovsky, *Writing and Fantasy in Proust: La Place de la Madeleine*, translated by Carol Mastrangelo Bové (Lincoln: University of Nebraska Press, 1986), p. 62.

9. Doubrovsky, *Writing and Fantasy in Proust*, p. 114.

10. Ellie Ragland-Sullivan, *Jacques Lacan and the Philosophy of Psychoanalysis* (Urbana: University of Illinois Press, 1986), p. 251.

11. Georges Bataille, *Erotism: Death and Sensuality*, translated by May Dalwood (San Francisco: City Lights, 1986), p. 86.

12. Emile Durkheim, *Suicide: A Study in Sociology*, translated by John A. Spaulding and George Simpson (New York: Free Press, 1951), p. 247.

13. Thomas Mann, *Essays of Three Decades*, translated by H. T. Lowe Porter (New York: Knopf, 1948), p. 381.

14. Mann, *Essays of Three Decades*, p. 254.

15. Bersani, *A Future for Astyanax*, p. 166.

16. Bersani, *A Future for Astyanax*, p. 314.

17. Fyodor Dostoevsky, *Notes from Underground* (1864), translated by Andrew R. MacAndrew (New York: New American Library, 1961), p. 203.

18. Dostoevsky, *Notes*, p. 113.

19. Dostoevsky, *Notes*, p. 112

20. Dostoevsky, *Notes*, p. 118

21. Lionel Trilling, *Beyond Culture* (New York: Viking, 1965), pp. 57–58.

22. Trilling, *Beyond Culture*, p. 90.

23. Trilling, *Beyond Culture*, p. 150.

24. Milan Kundera, *The Unbearable Lightness of Being*, translated by Michael Henry Heim (New York: Harper and Row, 1985), p. 111.

25. Kundera, *Unbearable Lightness*, p. 35.

26. Kundera, *Unbearable Lightness*, p. 221.

27. Annette Baier, "The Ambiguous Limits of Desire," in Joel Marks, ed., *The Ways of Desire* (Chicago: Precedent, 1986), p. 58.

28. Quoted in Albert Camus, *The Rebel* (Harmondsworth, Middlesex: Penguin, 1965), p. 15.

29. Juliet Mitchell, *Psychoanalysis and Feminism: Freud, Reich, Laing and Women* (New York: Random House, 1974), p. 304.

30. Andrew Benjamin, ed., *The Lyotard Reader* (Oxford: Basil Blackwell, 1989), p. 114.

31. Jean Baudrillard, *Selected Writings*, edited by Mark Poster (Stanford: Stanford University Press, 1988), p. 45.

32. See René Girard, *Deceit, Desire and the Novel* (Baltimore: Johns Hopkins University Press, 1966), chapter 1.

1. Conrad's *Heart of Darkness:* Allegory of Enlightenment

1. Ross Murfin, ed., *Heart of Darkness Casebook* (New York: St. Martin's, 1989), p. 222.

2. Ian Watt, "*Heart of Darkness* and Nineteenth-Century Thought," *Partisan Review* 14(1):110, 1978.

3. Herbert Marcuse, *Eros and Civilization* (New York: Vintage, 1955), p. 52.

4. Quoted in Edward Said, *Joseph Conrad and the Fiction of Autobiography* (Cambridge: Harvard University Press, 1966), p. 148.

5. There is a third kind of reason, the reason of the bureaucracy, embodied, for instance, in the figure of the manager of the Central Station.

Michael Levenson reads *Heart of Darkness* as an allegory of the bureaucratic corruption of reason under the aegis of imperialism. Following Weber, Levenson characterizes the bureaucrat in the following incriminating manner. "Lacking both reverence for tradition and hope of revolutionary change, content to sustain the prevailing hierarchy, committed to discipline and routine, willing to follow directives from above but incapable of devising independent initiatives, the Bureaucrat has history on his side and can wait patiently while his dominion extends into every aspect of contemporary life." "The Value of Facts in the *Heart of Darkness*," *Nineteenth-Century Fiction* (December 1985):268. Kurtz, in Levenson's reading, is a contradictory embodiment of the bureaucratic and the charismatic, another Weberian category. Marlow, the practical moralist, provides no redeeming perspective, because his judgments and actions are not based on general principles and actions. It would seem on this reading that any attempt to overcome the increasing hegemony of an instrumental reason is an exercise in futility.

6. Joseph Conrad, "An Outpost of Progress," in *Tales of Unrest* (Harmondsworth, Middlesex: Penguin, 1978–1987), p. 95. I think Conrad means no more than a realistic representation of life in the jungle wilderness, where disease and poverty are present. He doesn't mean to justify the European ambition to conquer Africa: he cannot mean to do so, since he exposes European incomprehension of Africa and its interest in exploiting it.

7. Conrad, "An Outpost of Progress," p. 88.

8. Sigmund Freud, *Standard Edition of the Complete Psychological Works* (24 vols.), edited and translated by James Strachey (London: Hogarth Press, 1953–1974; New York: Macmillan), 17:241 (hereafter cited as *S.E.*).

9. Theodor Adorno and Max Horkheimer, *Dialectic of Enlightenment* (New York: Seabury Press, 1944, 1969), p. 54.

10. Adorno and Horkheimer, *Dialectic of Enlightenment*, pp. 68–69.

11. Quoted in Patrick Brantlinger, "*Heart of Darkness:* Anti-Imperialism, Racism, or Impressionism?," *Criticism* (Fall 1985):363–85.

12. Benita Parry, *Conrad and Imperialism* (London: Macmillan, 1983), p. 23.

13. Freud, *S.E.*, 17:235.

14. Freud, *S.E.*, 17:235–36.

15. Steven Marcus, *Freud and the Culture of Psychoanalysis* (New York: Norton, 1987), p. 172.

16. Conrad, "An Outpost of Progress," p. 100.

2. The Art of Ambivalence: Mann's *Death in Venice*

1. Marcel Proust, *Remembrance of Things Past*, translated by C. K. Scott Moncrieff (New York: Random House, 1924–1934), 1:448.

2. Erich Heller, *The Ironic German: A Study of Thomas Mann* (Boston: Little, Brown, 1958), pp. 113–14, 101.

3. D. H. Lawrence, "German Books: Thomas Mann," in E. D. McDonald, ed., *Phoenix: The Posthumous Papers of D. H. Lawrence* (New York: Viking, 1950), p. 312.

4. A. E. Dyson, "The Stranger God: *Death in Venice*," *Critical Quarterly* 13:5–20, 1971.

5. Kenneth Burke, *Counter-Statement* (Berkeley: University of California Press, 1968), p. xii.

6. Burke, *Counter-Statement*, p. 106.

3. D. H. Lawrence and the Tyranny of Desire

1. D. H. Lawrence, *Psychoanalysis and the Unconscious* (1921) and *Fantasia of the Unconscious* (1922) (New York: Viking, 1960–1967), p. 5.

2. Lawrence, *Psychoanalysis* and *Fantasia*, p. 8. René Girard's conception of the oedipal drama is remarkably similar to Lawrence's, though Girard makes no acknowledgment of it. "The incest wish, the patricide wish, do not belong to the child but spring from the mind of the adult, the model. In the Oedipus myth it is the oracle that puts such ideas into Laius' head, long before Oedipus himself was capable of entertaining any ideas at all. Freud invokes the same ideas, which are no more valid than Laius'. The son is always the last to learn that what he desires is incest and patricide, and it is the hypocritical adult who undertakes to enlighten him in this matter." René Girard, *Violence and the Sacred* (Baltimore: Johns Hopkins University Press, 1977), p. 175. Girard's critique of Freud is based on his theory that desire is not directed toward a specific object, but is rather an imitation of what someone else desires: "The mimetic process detaches desire from any predetermined object, whereas the Oedipus complex fixes desire on the maternal object. The mimetic concept eliminates all conscious knowledge of patricide-incest, and even all desire for it as such; the Freudian proposition, by contrast, is based entirely on a consciousness of this desire" (180). If the son desires the mother, it is only because he is imitating his father's desire.

3. Lawrence, *Psychoanalysis* and *Fantasia*, p. 154.

Notes

4. Lawrence, *Psychoanalysis* and *Fantasia*, p. 87.
5. Lawrence, *Psychoanalysis* and *Fantasia*, pp. 112–13.
6. Lawrence, *Psychoanalysis* and *Fantasia*, p. 60.
7. From the point of view of social history, *The Rainbow* is a "narrative" of three generations of Brangwens which describes a "progress" from an original condition of agrarian harmony between man and nature (first generation), through the industrial revolution (second generation), and into the modern world (third generation).
8. Michel Foucault, *The History of Sexuality* (1976) (New York: Vintage, 1980), p. 157.
9. Foucault, *History of Sexuality*, p. 155.
10. Lawrence, *Psychoanalysis* and *Fantasia*, p. 220.
11. D. H. Lawrence, *Apocalypse* (1930) (New York: Viking, 1966), p. 200.

4. What Dowell Knew: A Reading of Ford's *The Good Soldier*

1. Eight years later, Hemingway published *The Sun Also Rises*, a novel about an impotent hero whose impotence marks his integrity in a world gone dissolute. I don't mean to suggest that Dowell is a comparable figure of integrity in *The Good Soldier*, only that a post-Freudian moralizing about the sexual deficiencies of a character may be irrelevant to the theme of the novel, as it would be to the theme of *The Sun Also Rises*.
2. Mark Schorer, "An Interpretation," introduction to *The Good Soldier* (New York: Random House, 1985), p. vii.
3. Michael Levenson, "Character in *The Good Soldier*," *Twentieth-Century Literature* (Winter 1984):383.
4. Levenson, "Character in *The Good Soldier*," 384–85.
5. The distortions consist (in Moser's view) in the fact that Violet was not the empty chatterbox, the piece of paper Dowell reduces her to, nor was Elsie the cruel, frigid creature that Leonora is meant to be. Thomas Moser, *The Life in the Fiction of Ford Madox Ford* (Princeton: Princeton University Press, 1980).
6. This puts Ford's doctrine of Impressionism in a nutshell.
7. When Dowell dismisses Florence as a "piece of paper," he is distinguishing her moral nullity from the moral character of the others. But one wonders whether all the characters are not little more than paper, texts composed of vacuous talk.
8. If Dowell were a character in a D. H. Lawrence novel, his ignorance would be seen as a reflection of his bodiless character. Not to live in the body is not to truly know. Lawrence repudiates mind consciousness, because it is a false consciousness—and false because it is unembodied. No character in a Lawrence novel surpasses Dowell as an example of mind consciousness.
9. The Chaucerian word is appropriate here.

10. Sondra J. Stang, *Ford Madox Ford* (New York: Ungar, 1977), pp. 71–72.

11. Stang, *Ford*, p. 89.

12. Stang, *Ford*, p. 82.

13. The essay is one of the best we have on *The Good Soldier*, for it grasps what few essays on the novel seem to comprehend: the sexual and moral quandaries of men and women at a critical moment in the history of civilization. It refuses to be diverted by an excessive (and often sterile) preoccupation with the problematics of point of view.

14. Levenson, "Character in *The Good Soldier*," p. 376.

15. Levenson, "Character in *The Good Soldier*," pp. 382–83.

16. *Notes from Underground* provides an analogous prospect of unacknowledged compulsive desire.

17. *The Sun Also Rises* once again comes to mind with its poignant sense of the fleeting quality of all happiness. If *The Sun Also Rises* is not the saddest story, it is because an idea of value (incarnated in the grace and integrity of Jake Barnes) survives the devastations of the novel. It is difficult to say what is redeemable in *The Good Soldier*.

18. Ford Madox Ford, *Parade's End* (New York: Knopf, 1966), p. 638.

5. Family, Incest, and Transcendence in Brontë's *Wuthering Heights*

1. Tony Tanner, *Adultery in the Novel* (Baltimore: Johns Hopkins University Press, 1979), p. 97.

2. Tanner, *Adultery in the Novel*, pp. 97–98.

3. Tanner, *Adultery in the Novel*, pp. 97–98.

4. Tanner, *Adultery in the Novel*, p. 89.

5. See Bersani, *A Future for Astyanax*, pp. 189–229.

6. Sandra Gilbert and Susan Gubar, *The Madwoman in the Attic: The Woman Writer and the Nineteenth-Century Literary Imagination* (New Haven: Yale University Press, 1979). Gilbert and Gubar have argued that women writers have been excluded from the modern "canon" by its patriarchal proprietors. It would be impossible to make a comparable argument for the nineteenth-century novel in England. Jane Austen, George Eliot, and the Brontës (Emily in particular) have always been among the chief glories in the English tradition. I prefer "tradition" to "canon" because tradition suggests change as well as continuity, whereas the canon is fixed and inalterable. The introduction of the words canon and canonicity in the recent debates about literary value has, I think, distorted the issues. Perhaps there is another explanation for the absence of women writers from the modernist great tradition.

Could it be that for all the complaints and the truth about the repressiveness (for women in particular) of the bourgeois family structure, it was the central presence of the family in Victorian society that empowered the female imagination even in the rebellion? With its loss of authority in the modern world, the female imagination had to be "enfranchised" in what became the dominant condition of modern life for the modern literary imagination: alienation. We see the modern alienated, desiring woman in the work of Virginia Woolf and Jean Rhys, and later in Doris Lessing, but the alienated desiring woman, cut loose from family life, has not established an imaginative authority comparable to that of Kurtz and Aschenbach. The process of imaginative enfranchisement takes time and we are beginning to see it in the work of feminist literature and criticism.

7. See Northrop Frye, *An Anatomy of Criticism* (Princeton: Princeton University Press, 1957), p. 304.

8. Bersani, *A Future for Astyanax*, p. 206.

9. Dorothy Van Ghent, *The English Novel: Form and Function* (New York: Holt, Rinehart and Winston, 1953), p. 153.

10. Van Ghent, *The English Novel*, pp. 169–70.

11. Van Ghent, *The English Novel*, p. 171.

12. Hindley's wife Frances is also an outsider, a shadowy vessel for the birth of Hareton, who is pure Earnshaw. She is a biological necessity and a dramatic embarrassment. Emily Brontë's incestuous imagination brings her on and off the stage (Frances dies soon after the birth of Hareton) with the greatest dispatch.

13. See Eric Salomon, "The Incest Theme in *Wuthering Heights*," *Nineteenth-Century Fiction* 14:80–83, June 1959.

14. Thomas Moser, "What is the Matter with Emily Jane? Conflicting Impulses in *Wuthering Heights*," in *Wuthering Heights—Text, Sources, Criticism* (New York: Harcourt, Brace and World, 1962), p. 226.

15. Hillis Miller, *The Disappearance of God* (Cambridge: Harvard University Press, 1963), p. 200.

16. M. H. Abrams, *Natural Supernaturalism: Tradition and Revolution in Romantic Literature* (New York: Norton, 1971), p. 165.

17. Moser, "What is the Matter with Emily Jane?," pp. 1–19.

18. Miller, *The Disappearance of God*, p. 200.

19. Bersani, *A Future for Astyanax*, p. 201.

20. Marianne Hirsch, *The Mother/Daughter Plot* (Bloomington: Indiana University Press, 1989), pp. 11–12.

21. See Mitchell, *Psychoanalysis and Feminism*, pp. 377–81.

22. Mitchell, *Psychoanalysis and Feminism*, p. 375. Mitchell derives the phrase from Engels. "What is originally holy is what we have taken over from the animal kingdom—*the bestial.*" Engels to Marx, December 8, 1882, *Selected Correspondence* (1934 ed.), p. 406.

6. Desire and Its Discontents

1. Herbert Marcuse, *Eros and Civilization* (New York: Vintage, 1955), p. 52.

2. Richard Rorty, *Pragmatism's Freud: The Moral Disposition of Psychoanalysis*, edited by Joseph H. Smith and William Kerrigan (Baltimore: Johns Hopkins University Press, 1986), p. 11.

3. Rorty, *Pragmatism's Freud*, p. 23.

4. Carl Schorske, *Fin de Siècle Vienna: Politics and Culture* (New York: Knopf, 1980), p. 185.

5. Schorske, *Fin de Siècle Vienna*, p. 191.

6. Schorske, *Fin de Siècle Vienna*, pp. 202–3.

7. Freud, *S.E.*, 4:86.

8. Marcuse, *Eros and Civilization*, pp. 31–32.

9. Elizabeth Gaskell, *North and South*. 1854–55 (London: Penguin, 1970), p. 217.

10. The utopianism of desire had an earlier advocate in the 1930s and 1940s in the work of Wilhelm Reich, whose celebration of genital sexuality and the orgasm became a rallying cry for sexual radicalism. Reich, like Marcuse after him, tried to achieve a kind of synthesis of Freudianism and Marxism. One finds a renewed interest in Reich in the 1960s, but he is not the seminal figure that Marcuse or, for that matter, Brown was in the upheavals of the 1960s. Reich's stress on genital sexuality was regarded, from the standpoint of polymorphous perversity, as a species of repression. Reich is also theoretically less interesting than Marcuse or Brown. For an interesting critique of Reich from a Freudian point of view, see Mitchell, *Psychoanalysis and Feminism*, pp. 137–223.

11. Freud, *S.E.*, 16:322.

12. Marcuse, *Eros and Civilization*, p. 166.

13. Marcuse, *Eros and Civilization*, p. 168.

14. Marcuse, *Eros and Civilization*, p. 112.

15. Quoted in Erich Heller, *The Disinherited Mind* (Harmondsworth, Middlesex: Penguin, 1961), p. 121.

16. Marcuse, *Eros and Civilization*, p. 11.

17. Norman O. Brown, *Life Against Death* (New York: Modern Library, 1959), p. 7.

18. Brown, *Life Against Death*, p. 176.

19. Brown, *Life Against Death*, p. 181.

20. In an extraordinary book, *Christ and Nietzsche: An Essay in Poetic Wisdom* (London: Staples Press, 1948), G. Wilson Knight discovers Dionysus within Christ himself.

21. Norman O. Brown, *Love's Body* (New York: Vintage, 1966), p. 216.

22. Brown, *Love's Body*, p. 215.

23. Sigmund Freud, *Beyond the Pleasure Principle* (1920) (New York: Norton, 1961), p. 47.

24. Freud, *Beyond the Pleasure Principle*, p. 31.

25. Freud, *Beyond the Pleasure Principle*, p. 33.

26. Sigmund Freud, *Civilization and Its Discontents* (1930) (New York: Norton, 1962), p. 103.

27. Freud, *Civilization and Its Discontents*, p. 104.

28. Gilles Deleuze and Felix Guattari, *Anti-Oedipus: Capitalism and Schizophrenia* (Minneapolis: University of Minnesota Press, 1983), pp. 1–2.

29. Lionel Trilling, *Sincerity and Authenticity* (Cambridge: Harvard University Press, 1971–72), p. 145.

30. Trilling, *Sincerity and Authenticity*, p. 169.

31. Trilling, *Sincerity and Authenticity*, pp. 171–72.

32. Trilling, *Sincerity and Authenticity*, p. 166.

33. Trilling, *Sincerity and Authenticity*, p. 170.

34. Foucault, *History of Sexuality*, vol. 1, p. 23.

35. Foucault, *History of Sexuality*, vol. 1, p. 155.

36. Foucault writes the kind of philosophical history that frustrates historians and readers of history of empiricist persuasion. Foucault simply does not provide the kind of evidence and argumentation to sustain a historical thesis. But his speculations, when they seem to strike a truth, provoke readers to adduce evidences from their own readings and understandings.

37. Freud, *S.E.*, 16:351.

38. Freud, *S.E.*, 14:58.

39. Freud, *S.E.*, 14:59.

40. Freud, *S.E.*, 9:192.

41. Steven Marcus, *The Other Victorians* (New York: Basic Books, 1966), p. 284.

42. Freud, *S.E.*, 11:188.

43. Freud, *S.E.*, 17:251.

44. Freud, *S.E.*, 13:233.

45. Freud, *S.E.*, 13:234.

46. Freud, *S.E.*, 9:199.

47. Paul Rabinow, ed., *The Foucault Reader* (New York: Pantheon, 1984), p. 340.

48. Steven Marcus, "Conceptions of the Self in Freud and Recent Psychoanalyses," unpublished manuscript.

49. Steven Marcus, *Freud and the Culture of Psychoanalysis*, (New York: Norton, 1987) pp. 187–89.

50. Ann Beattie, *Chilly Scenes of Winter* (New York: Doubleday, 1976), p. 202.

7. The Freudian Narrative and the Case of Jacques Lacan

1. Ellie Ragland-Sullivan, *Jacques Lacan and the Philosophy of Psychoanalysis* (Urbana: University of Illinois Press, 1987), p. 5.

2. Ragland-Sullivan, *Jacques Lacan*, pp. 271–72.

3. Jacques Lacan, *Four Fundamental Concepts*, translated by Alan Sher-

idan (London: Hogarth Press and the Institute of Psychoanalysis, 1977), p. 176.

4. Lacan, *Four Fundamental Concepts*, p. 31.

5. See Sigmund Freud, "Analysis: Terminable and Interminable" (1937), in *S.E.*, 23:216–53.

6. Stuart Schneiderman, *Jacques Lacan: The Death of an Intellectual Hero* (Cambrdige: Harvard University Press, 1983), p. 114.

7. Schneiderman, *Jacques Lacan*, p. 110.

8. Ragland-Sullivan, *Jacques Lacan*, p. 12.

9. Malcolm Bowie, *Freud, Proust and Lacan: Theory as Fiction* (Cambridge: Cambridge University Press, 1987), p. 123.

10. See Bowie, *Freud, Proust and Lacan*, p. 122.

11. Sigmund Freud, *The Ego and the Id* (1923), translated by Joan Riviere, revised by James Strachey (New York: Norton, 1962), p. 46.

12. Lacan, *Four Fundamental Concepts*, p. 24.

13. Bowie, *Freud, Proust and Lacan*, p. 118.

14. Ragland-Sullivan, *Jacques Lacan*, p. 15.

15. Ragland-Sullivan, *Jacques Lacan*, p. 77.

16. Lacan, *Four Fundamental Concepts*, p. 134.

17. Bowie, *Freud, Proust and Lacan*, p. 153.

18. See Ragland-Sullivan, *Jacques Lacan*, p. 62.

19. Ragland-Sullivan, *Jacques Lacan*, pp. 251–52.

20. Shoshana Felman, *Jacques Lacan and the Adventure of Insight: Psychoanalysis in Contemporary Culture* (Cambridge: Harvard University Press, 1987), pp. 48–49.

21. Felman, *Jacques Lacan and the Adventure of Insight*, p. 89.

22. Schneiderman, *Jacques Lacan*, p. 58.

23. Schneiderman, *Jacques Lacan*, p. 85

24. Felman, *Jacques Lacan and the Adventure of Insight*, p. 144.

25. Felman, *Jacques Lacan and the Adventure of Insight*, p. 131.

26. Felman, *Jacques Lacan and the Adventure of Insight*, p. 137.

27. Roy Schafer, *On Narrative*, edited by W. J. T. Mitchell (Chicago: University of Chicago Press, 1980–81), p. 44.

8. "Postmodern" Meditations on the Self: The Work of Philip Roth and Don DeLillo

1. Philip Roth, *Deception* (New York: Simon and Schuster, 1990), p. 103.

2. Don DeLillo, *Americana* (Boston: Houghton Mifflin, 1971), p. 28.

3. Don DeLillo, *The Names* (New York: Random House, 1982), p. 200.

4. Saul Friedlander, *Reflections on Nazism* (New York: Harper and Row, 1984), p. 25.

5. Friedlander, *Reflections on Nazism*, p. 26.

9. Desire and the Self

1. Virginia Woolf, *A Room of One's Own* (1928) (Harmondsworth, Middlesex: Penguin, 1963–73), pp. 69–70.

2. Alexander Nehamas, *Nietzsche: Life as Literature* (Cambridge: Harvard University Press, 1985), p. 183.

3. Thomas Hardy, *Jude the Obscure* (New York: Norton, 1978), p. 167.

4. Hardy, *Jude the Obscure,* p. 171.

5. Nehamas, *Nietzsche,* p. 48.

6. Nehamas, *Nietzsche,* p. 47.

❧ Index

191

117, 120; "Repression," 117; Sartre and, 128; on self-knowledge, 133; on self-mastery, 136; on sexual desire, 136; on sexuality, 119-20, 132-37; sexual morality and, 133-34; social change, 116; social theory and, 115-16; *Totem and Taboo*, 120; utopianism and, 154-55
Friedländer, Saul, 169-70
Fromm, Erich, 115
Future for Astyanax, A (Bersani), 2

Garcia Marquez, Gabriel: *One Hundred Years of Solitude*, 99
Gaskell, Elizabeth: *North and South*, 97, 118-19
Gay liberation, 173
Gertler, Max, 74
Gide, André, 8
Gilbert, Sandra, 98, 184n6
Girard, René, 20, 182n2
Goethe, Johann Wolfgang von: *Elective Affinities*, 97
Good Soldier, The (Ford), 79-94, 184nn13, 17
Guattari, Felix, 144; *Anti-Oedipus*, 126-28
Gubar, Susan, 98, 184n6

Hardy, Thomas: *Jude the Obscure*, 175-76
Heart of Darkness (Conrad), 19, 20, 23-36, 40-43, 122; as allegory of bureaucracy, 181n5; revisionist views of, 32-33; *see also* Conrad, Joseph
Hegel, Georg Wilhelm Friedrich, 120-21, 153-54
Heller, Eric, 50-51
Hemingway, Ernest: *The Sun Also Rises*, 183n1, 184n17
Herbert, George, 65
"History of the Psychoanalytic Movement, A" (Freud), 132
History of Sexuality, The (Foucault), 69, 128, 130-31
Home: desire for, 110-11, 153

Homosexuality, 53-55, 73
Horkheimer, Max, 30-31
Hueffer, Elsie, 83
Hume, David, 1, 21, 179n3
Hunt, Violet, 83

Id: ego and, 145-46; Sartre's view of, 128-29
Identity, 171; desire and, 13; family and, 109; reason and, 11; religion and, 108; sexual, 72-73, 138; union and, 108-9
Imagination: contemporary, 156; desire and, 6, 7, 45, 114, 174; female, 185n6; modernist, 9; postmodernism and, 9-10, 158-59, 163-64; Roth and, 160-64; sexual, 75
Impressionism, 82, 91, 93
Incest, 99-103, 107, 109-10, 111, 182n.2
independence: of the individual, 68-69; *see also* Autonomy
Individuality: in family, 98; incest and, 99-102; in *Wuthering Heights*, 103

Jane Eyre (C. Brönte), 173-74, 176
Jaspers, Karl, 79
Joyce, James, 148
Jude the Obscure (Hardy), 175-76

Kafka, Franz, 8
Kangaroo (Lawrence), 74
Keats, John, 152
Kitsch, 169-70
Kohut, Heinz, 139-40
Kristeva, Julia: "The Ethics of Linguistics," 2
Kundera, Milan: *The Unbearable Lightness of Being*, 14-16

Lacan, Jacques, 6, 7, 143-52; on desire for cure, 151-52; on death, 151-52; on ego psychology, 143, 151; Freud and, 143-47, 151-52, 155; on love and desire, 151; on pleasure principle, 144; on psychoanalytic status of poets, 150-51; on